"This delightful, inspiring, and practical book can help transform anyone's meditation practice from a struggle to a joy. Based on years of experience as a gifted psychologist and meditation teacher, Dr. Morgan lucidly shows us how to avoid the pitfalls that make meditation unnecessarily difficult, while finding ways to harness our surprisingly natural capacity for clarity and ease. Full of wisdom and compassion, it's a must-read for all who wish to deepen and enliven their meditation practice and live a richer, happier, more connected life." —Ronald D. Siegel, PsyD, author of *The Mindfulness Solution*

"Have you ever wanted to know the secret of a happy meditator? With disarming candor and delightful humor, psychologist Bill Morgan shares hard-won insights gleaned from over forty years on the cushion. He shows us how to bring the qualities of play, delight, gratitude, warmth, and tenderness to mindfulness meditation practice, while remaining rooted in the ancient teachings of the Buddha. This book has the power to liberate the hearts of both novice and seasoned meditators. Spare yourself unnecessary struggle and read it now!" —Christopher Germer, PhD, author of *The Mindful Path to Self-Compassion*

"In *The Meditator's Dilemma*, Bill Morgan offers us some of the many fruits of his long meditation experience. His firsthand experience of grappling with the dilemmas that confront most meditators helps illuminate some of the common difficulties and struggles we encounter on the path. In this very helpful book, he offers a wide array of skillful suggestions that allow for a natural and more easeful unfolding of our insight and understanding." —Joseph Goldstein, author of *Mindfulness: A Practical Guide to Awakening*

"A noteworthy reevaluation of one Westerner's initial enthusiasm over mindfulness meditation. William Morgan shares his frustrations and his solutions in this timely work." —Mark Epstein MD, author of *The Trauma of Everyday Life*

THE MEDITATOR'S DILEMMA

An Innovative Approach to
Overcoming Obstacles and
Revitalizing Your Practice

BILL MORGAN

SHAMBHALA Boulder 2016

Shambhala Publications, Inc.
4720 Walnut Street
Boulder, Colorado 80301
www.shambhala.com

9 8 7 6 5 4 3 2 1

First Edition
Printed in the United States of America

♾ This edition is printed on acid-free paper that meets the
American National Standards Institute Z39.48 Standard.
♻ This book is printed on 30% postconsumer recycled paper.
For more information please visit www.shambhala.com.

Distributed in the United States by Penguin Random House LLC
and in Canada by Random House of Canada Ltd

Designed by Greta D. Sibley

Library of Congress Cataloging-in-Publication Data
Names: Morgan, Bill (Psychologist)
Title: The meditator's dilemma: an innovative approach to overcoming
    obstacles and revitalizing your practice / Bill Morgan.
Description: First Edition. | Boulder: Shambhala, 2016. | Includes
    bibliographical references.
Identifiers: LCCN 2015029253 | ISBN 9781611802481 (pbk.: alk. paper)
Subjects: LCSH: Meditation—Buddhism.
Classification: LCC BQ5612 .M67 2016 | DDC 294.3/4435—dc23 LC
    record available at http://lccn.loc.gov/2015029253

For my father,
who loved hard
and died young

We must risk delight. We can do without pleasure, but not delight. Not enjoyment. We must have the stubbornness to accept our gladness in the ruthless furnace of this world.

—Jack Gilbert

CONTENTS

APPRECIATIONS

MUCH GRATITUDE TO:

Joseph Goldstein, who, since 1978, has supported and inspired me through six years of silent retreats at the Insight Meditation Society and Forest Refuge.

Numerous pioneer teachers who have dedicated their lives to bringing these practices to the West, and who kindled me in the process.

Fellow members of the Institute for Meditation and Psychotherapy, especially Chris Germer, Ron Siegel, Paul Fulton, Jan Surrey, Charles Styron, Trudy Goodman, Susan Pollak, Tom Pedulla, Sara Lazar, Chris Willard, and Nayla Khoury for their enduring support over the past thirty years.

Bill O'Hanlon, who always believed there was a book forthcoming.

Cindy Barrilleaux, who was there from the beginning; she was persevering in keeping the work grounded and lifting me during darker moments.

Gordon Thomas, who, in the latter stages of the project, helped greatly with consolidation and flow.

Jeanne Ann Whittington, a dear friend who reviewed several iterations of the book with great care and insight.

All of the clients and fellow meditators who inspired me more than they can know.

My dear sister Melanie: steady, loving, and true.

My radiant partner and coteacher, Susan, who pours love into everything she touches and inspires me endlessly.

INTRODUCTION

IT IS DARK AND COLD in the mountains as I shuffle to the meditation hall in my dark robe at three thirty in the morning. I'm still half asleep, but my first thought before settling into meditation is, *Maybe this will be the day I have an important breakthrough.*

The atmosphere in the hall is tense, and the teacher's assistant has already begun her ominous, slow pacing in front of the row of meditators. She is carrying a stick the length of a yardstick but wider and thicker. Definitely thicker. This woman is prepared to strike anyone who appears sleepy or uninspired. Of course, there is a certain arbitrariness to her assessment, so one can never relax.

I am twenty years old and have just come across the country during my summer break, highly motivated to find something deep and true, a life-changing insight that would surely reorient my life after the sudden death of my dear father. Numb, shocked, and disenchanted with once-satisfying activities, I am struggling to recapture a sense of purpose. I had read accounts of great breakthroughs in meditation following deep personal loss. If I stay unrelentingly with my meditation practice, perhaps my life will undergo a radical transformation.

The tap on my shoulder comes as a surprise, as does my momentary unwillingness to bow to the woman standing before me. I remind myself that she is only doing this for the benefit of my practice. She wants only to raise my energy and dedication to a higher level. Remembering that life is short, I bow. She reaches to find the soft tissue above my shoulder blade, of which, being thin, I have precious little. Who can blame her if, in the dark, she misses and strikes bone, the stick breaking in half with the force of the strike, one piece crashing into the altar twenty feet away and knocking over a small Buddha statue. She strides to the back of the altar to retrieve another stick and returns to strike my other shoulder harder than the first. *There is no time for tears like these,* I think. But they do not stop flowing.

The year was 1972. Buddhist psychology and mindfulness were landing in earnest on Western shores, and I attempted to find solace and freedom through meditation. I rode this wave with dedication in those early days, exploring a variety of traditions. Over the next ten years, I would spend six months in a Trappist monastery, a summer at a Zen center, nine months at a Tibetan meditation center, and two three-month periods in retreats at the Insight Meditation Society in Massachusetts.

My choice of intensive environments in which to practice was reinforced by the teaching methods of the times, which actively encouraged a version of the hero's journey. Fiery determination and fierce effort were expected in those days. I was on board with that and believed that my inability to have a transformative breakthrough was due to my lack of diligence. The solution was to work still harder.

I did just that when, in 1984, I was invited to a three-month, very intensive meditation retreat with a teacher named Sayadaw U Pandita from Burma. It comprised daily interviews and incessant reminders to meditators of our laziness and the necessity of making sustained effort in order to attain enlightenment. Knowing that I was going to enter graduate school after the retreat fueled my determination. I worked feverishly, beating my head against an imagined wall in the hope of becoming enlightened. On one occasion, I thought I had broken through the wall, only to find that the neighboring cell was equally dry and humorless.

For many years I had been hesitant to write about this sobering aspect of meditation practice. Who wants to hear about the resistances and struggles involved, about misconceptions, missteps, and unmet expectations? Who wants to read a "self-hell" book?

Several events contributed to my change of heart. My graduate research, completed in 1990, focused on progress in meditation. As part of this project, I interviewed many practitioners, and this yielded a consistent and surprising result. Every meditator I interviewed struggled extensively with a sense of striving, failure, and disappointment in meditation. Each one had difficulty establishing a regular practice. I discovered I was not alone.

Since then, over the years of teaching meditation and working with clients in my psychotherapy practice, I have come to see that my struggles, striving, and self-defeating styles of practice are common among Western students. Many others deal with a sense of frustration and ineffectiveness in their meditation or have been unable to apply the practice in daily life situations. In fact, I suspect that a silent majority of meditators struggle and feel alone in their struggle. Perhaps they fail to report the extent of their sense of inadequacy to their teachers or fellow practitioners out of a desire to be seen as motivated or accomplished.

My suspicions were confirmed when, several years ago, I wrote an article titled "Resistance in Meditation." In it I characterize the practice of meditation as a series of narcissistic injuries and disappointments. Afterward, I heard from many practitioners who resonated with this sense of struggle and who encouraged me to explore this topic further.

Despite my well-grounded sense that most meditators struggle, I could not have written this book had I not experienced a series of insights in my practice. The most pivotal revealed that the way I had been practicing was largely ineffective because it was pressured, forced, and filled with self-judgment. This led me to radically reevaluate, dismantle, and reorganize every aspect of my practice.

Motivated to reinvent meditation as a deeply personal, intimate practice, I began to consider other, possibly more creative ways for holding my attention. Having given myself permission to experiment with approaches outside the box, I discovered new methods of reflection and practice that were actually enlivening. At this juncture, meditation began to unfold in new and transformative ways.

Having made these discoveries, I thought they could benefit others. Along with my partner, Susan, a long-term meditator and psychotherapist, I have since been teaching these new approaches in retreats and with individual clients with striking results. It is one thing to experience a personal epiphany, and quite another to have it verified by the subjective reports of others. It is this wider validation that has encouraged me to further share these revitalizing approaches to meditation. Without the positive feedback of students and clients, this boat would not have left the dock.

This book is written for new meditators as well as the many experienced practitioners who have experienced similar struggles. Chapter 1 deals with what I consider to be the elephant in the meditation room: common pitfalls in meditation, misguided assumptions and unbalanced styles of practice, dysfunctional and destructive attitudes in meditation that can persist for many years, and the hard-to-notice toxic filters through which we practice. While some degree of sweat and tears must be endured in any growth process, suffering in meditation is often unnecessary. I know this territory intimately.

Chapter 2 addresses the cultural dispositions that make it difficult for Westerners to practice meditation. Traditional meditation instructions arose at a particular time and in a specific context very different from that in which most of us practice today.

Chapter 3 introduces a context for framing meditation practice suitable to our cultural setting. Relatively little attention has been given to setting the stage for meditation. Perhaps this is not necessary for practitioners raised in a culture where traditional practices and faith in them have been present for millennia. However, in our culture, this is the most overlooked and underappreciated aspect of meditation teaching. I call this the "inner holding environment."

Chapter 4 considers the importance of personal meaning making in meditation. Traditional instructions tend to minimize the personal in favor of universal truths. Because we live in a culture that emphasizes self-development and enhancement, this cultural predisposition needs to be incorporated into meditation instruction. Westerners need a unique and personal gateway into these practices.

The next section of the book focuses on skills that facilitate meditation. I liken this to a sports experience I had as a child. When I was eleven years old, I switched from baseball to golf as my primary sport. I knew how to hold and swing a bat, so I assumed that a golf club wouldn't give me difficulty. Thus I never felt the need to take a lesson. After struggling with slices and hooks for several years, I took a single lesson that improved my golf game dramatically. It turned out that I had been holding the club incorrectly, which had negatively affected the distance and trajectory of the ball.

It is the same in meditation. We need new skills. Consciously exploring the inner landscape in meditation requires unique sensitivities. Just as in my experience with golf, if you do not learn how to "hold" your meditation practice, the distance and trajectory of your meditation will be disappointing. We need a new framework for our practice that invites increasing intimacy with the inner landscape of our experience. This section explores how to create this supportive container. The lack of this holding container is largely responsible for why many Westerners get lost in their efforts to meditate.

Chapters 5 through 8 are devoted to each aspect of creating this inner holding environment: settling the body, establishing the mood, arousing affect in a number of ways, finding personally meaningful ways to engage with the practice. Each of these contributes to the foundation for meditation.

Having developed a lush and meaningful holding environment, the second half of the book invites those who want to, to advance their meditation into the adventurous worlds of concentration, open-awareness, and inquiry practices. Here light is shed on common pitfalls of these realms. Concentration can be daunting and exasperating for Westerners. Because interest—not striving—is the mother of concentration, this section introduces playful and creative ways of bypassing striving. Meditation "games," offered in these chapters, also enhance engagement in the inquiry process.

Having direct experience with enlivening meditation practice is pivotal. Thinking about how it feels to gaze at the waters of the ocean on a favorite beach is not the same as physically being there. Reflecting on the benefits of meditation does not substitute for its actual taste. With this in mind, guided meditation exercises are offered throughout this book. Audio versions of many of these practices are available at http://www.shambhala.com/the-meditator-s-dilemma.html and at www.billandsusan.net/meditatorsdilemma.

Rethinking meditation alone will not lead to an enriched and sustainable relationship with practice. Only by trying a new approach a few times and evaluating its effectiveness versus a previous method of practice can we make the necessary assessments and adjustments. The Buddha urged others to consider his words carefully, to contemplate, to meditate, to draw their own conclusions based on personal investigation. This spirit is captured in the Pali word *ehipassiko,* which means "come and see for yourself." It is in that spirit that I invite you to try these exercises. While they have been designed to revitalize your meditation practice, you must evaluate them for yourself.

It took a long time for meditation practice to bear fruit in my life. I'd like you to suffer less than I did and to find joy in meditation sooner. It is my sincere wish that this book will put the wind in your sails, so that your mindfulness practice becomes more meaningful and satisfying at every stage in the journey.

PART ONE

THE WESTERN MEDITATOR'S DILEMMA

There are two kinds of light—the glow that illuminates, and the glare that obscures.

—James Thurber

1

THE
STRIVING
PROBLEM

MOST OF US KNOW THE FEELING of being deeply alive and in the moment, captured by a meaningful activity or poignant interaction. Even if it comes rarely, the experience is so palpable that when you remember it, you can almost feel it all over again. Perhaps it comes when you are outdoors in an evening, completely entranced by a beautiful sunset; or when you experience a sweet connection with a dear friend; or perhaps you've experienced that vibrant sense when you are caught up in gardening or spending time with a child. When was the last time you entered into a creative act in which you were fully absorbed, when time seemed to be suspended? Surely two hallmarks of this elusive state we call happiness are these viscerally experienced moments of joy and contentment.

What if it were possible to experience these feelings more frequently and at will, even when clouds block the sunset, mosquitoes buzz you in the garden, and your friend cancels on you? In fact, through mindfulness meditation, you can do just that by going beneath the distractions and turbulence in your mind to a deeper, more engaging, and peaceful experience. In time, one can access this state with relative ease, attaining it comfortably within minutes.

The possibility of evoking these feelings through mindfulness practice often surprises people. Considering how long I struggled in meditation, it was a wonderful revelation to me as well. The primary emphasis in most instruction is upon repeatedly returning the attention to the present moment of experience, with the implicit sense that positive states and insights will arise from that core discipline. Do that, the teaching argues, and good things are sure to follow.

It took me twenty-five years to admit to myself that, in actuality, good things rarely followed. At that point, out of frustration, I reconsidered this core instruction and the manner in which I was practicing and took an honest inventory of the effects the practice had yielded in my life. For the longest time, I had simply taken on faith that returning to the present moment of experience, and keeping the attention there, would yield documented results, not the least of which was unalloyed peace of mind. If this wasn't unfolding for me, I just needed to practice harder. I practiced with diligence despite the fact that the process was seldom heartfelt, resulting in a dry, cognitive experience of meditation practice. I frequently felt parched and barren, but I kept telling myself that if the drilling continued, I was sure to hit water.

This unrewarding persistence is frequently practiced by clients in psychotherapy as well. Even when there is no progress, when the client doesn't feel particularly understood, or when the connection with the therapist is not strong, the client imagines it is his or her fault and keeps grinding away in this ineffective scenario. I kept grinding away in an unsatisfying mindfulness practice, imagining either that I wasn't doing it right or that I had a huge storehouse of negativity that had to be cooked out through this unhappy meditation. Surely the light bulb would go on eventually if I kept this up. But the aha moments were few and fleeting. I did learn to be more aware and mindful, but I didn't feel better about myself or my quality of life. I wasn't happier. This practice of mindfulness was supposed to lead at least to more ease and well-being, but that wasn't happening for me. What was missing?

When the Buddha taught meditation, he spoke of the necessity of first building a raft that could take us across the seas of confusion and grasping and distraction to a clearer, less troubled shore. A vital component of that raft, he taught, was concentration. And an essential piece of the concentration was calm. Concentration was about creating a pleasant, contented port in the storm, a refuge beneath the turbulent currents at the surface of the water, down to a peaceful place, so tantalizingly near at hand yet largely inaccessible without training. Without calmness, the uncollected mind would be distracted and swept away by thoughts and feelings. A relaxed focus was necessary, so the mind could stay with its varied and subtle movements without getting lost. This is why concentration practices were used first and extensively in most Buddhist meditation traditions.

However, fifty years ago, when mindfulness practices came to our shores in earnest, we had access to the story of the Buddha's journey. An important breakthrough in his journey was the discovery that freedom could not be attained through focus on a single object. Concentration was necessary but not sufficient for liberation, which could be accomplished through open awareness mindfulness practices only. In this manner of meditating, the attention is allowed to move about from one object to another, presumably without being distracted. Concentration was viewed by the Buddha as an essential component of meditation, but also as only preliminary.

Therefore, the attitude of my dharma friends back in the seventies and eighties was, "Why waste time on a beginning practice?" We believed that the open-awareness practices being taught to us would lead to liberating insight into the true nature of the mind, which would in turn set us free. Wanting to go straight to the heart of the matter, we worked hard at open awareness practices and gave little attention to concentration.

In addition, concentration practices, in their stripped-down traditional forms, are not interesting enough for the Western meditation student in our high-stimulus culture. We are more drawn to the open-awareness practices because they invite variety and complexity. Following the flow of the sensations of the breath, called for in concentration practices, is frequently perceived as monotonous. At the beginning of a recent retreat, I asked who among the paricipants found the breath to be an engaging object of meditation, and only one person raised a hand. I asked her to say more about this, and she said, "I visualize the breath to be a Ferris wheel. On the inhalation the Ferris wheel goes up, and on the exhalation it comes back down. That makes it more interesting." I asked, "And if you don't do that, and just stay with the sensations of the breath?" "Deadly," she replied.

Concentration practices, therefore, have not been emphasized much in the West. Because concentration is quite weak culturally—we are a low-attention-span, hyperactive society—this is turning out to be an oversight. If you ask long-term meditation students what the weakest link in their mindfulness practice is, most will tell you it is the ability to stay with their unfolding experience in a calm and continuous way. That is the province of concentration, which is the backbone of mindfulness.

It took me a long time to acknowledge the lack of calm and stability in my meditation practice. Whatever insights arose were therefore sporadic and fleeting, overwhelmed by distraction and discouragement and doubt.

I decided that the obvious step was to practice concentration meditation, which involved following the flow of sensations of the breath exclusively. That is when I discovered how weak my concentration was. When you are moving attention from one object to another, which is the technique used in open-awareness practice, it can seem that the mind is more or less staying in the present moment. Concentration on a single object, however, reveals the holes in this "more or less" perspective very quickly. When there is only one object to attend to, the wandering mind is starkly revealed.

I worked hard at improving concentration and became increasingly frustrated, never quite capturing that promised experience of peace. Meditation felt tight, claustrophobic. At times I felt as if I were locked in a dark closet. I believed that if I had kept as many thoughts out of the mind as possible, I would eventually break out into a spacious, airy landscape. That never happened. The effort to concentrate created tension, and when I grew tired and relaxed my efforts, I was bombarded by an avalanche of thoughts that had been suppressed. Further, I was bored by the technique. So I was at an impasse again. Why was I unable to access the fruits of concentration practice—states of joy and calm—even after years of practice?

Many meditators share the same struggles, but I have not yet seen a support group for the mindfulness-challenged. Research on the meditation dropout rate is scant, but what evidence we have reveals that more than half of those who begin meditation stop at some point, and most longer-term meditators I meet admit to being intermittent in their practice. The majority of clients and students I have worked with have struggled to find satisfaction in their meditation. Many, like me, kept at it even when it was yielding little fruit. It is safe to say that the silent majority of meditators do not find much pleasure in their practice.

Why so little satisfaction? If it's true that for millennia in the East meditation has reportedly reduced suffering, is it possible that Westerners simply need a different approach that speaks to our conditioning and inclinations? I believe that is the case.

My exasperation led me to cast a wider net in the search for solution to my meditation difficulties. Once I got beyond my self-recrimination and imagined deficits, I pondered the following questions:

- What might be different about the Western disposition?
- What might serve as a segue to more meaningful and satisfying mindfulness practice for myself and others in our culture?
- Once articulated and identified, how could these insights be shared with others?

QUESTIONS FOR CONSIDERATION

Don't we have to work hard at anything before experiencing benefits?
Why should meditation be any different in this regard?

While it is true that we need to consistently practice a sport or an instrument, for example, in order to make progress, the question is, how much effort is actually helpful? Too much pressure to excel, either internally or from coaches or teachers, setting the bar overly high, excessive delayed gratification, goal orientation that fails to appreciate and enjoy present-moment experience—these can quickly spoil one's relationship with almost any activity. This is what I experienced in my early years of meditation.

Is it possible that your style was overly pushy and ultimately contributed to your degree of struggle with meditation?

While this is certainly true, my work with clients and students over the years, coupled with my extensive interviews with meditators during my doctoral research, suggests that excessive striving is a cultural proclivity with respect to meditation. Heroic effort was encouraged in both subtle and overt ways in the Zen, Theravadan, and Tibetan centers in which I practiced.

2

DIFFERENT
STROKES

THOUGH MANY of the pragmatic teachings of the Buddha are universal and timeless, the meditation instructions themselves were offered at a particular time and in a unique cultural context. As I continued to search for a solution to my own meditation struggles, I began to wonder about how the differences in Eastern and Western milieus might account for the magnitude of the difficulties I was encountering. I identified several discrepancies between these cultural orientations that yielded insights into my personal dilemmas.

The Locus of Happiness: Internal versus External

Carbon dating has determined that some of the rock carvings of humans sitting in full lotus position discovered in India and Tibet are more than five thousand years old. Even before the time of the Buddha, the path toward happiness was understood to be an inner journey. The Upanishads and Vedas taught that contemplative practice promised deeper, more meaningful states of mind. The spiritual heroes of the age were mystics and ascetic wanderers. A folk saying still common in Tibet states that "seeking happiness outside is like waiting for sunshine in a cave facing north."

In the pursuit of freedom for India, Mahatma Gandhi said:

The outward freedom that we shall attain will only be in exact proportion to the inward freedom to which we may have grown in a given moment. And if this is a correct view of freedom, our chief energy must be concentrated on achieving reform from within.[1]

Western culture is clearly not contemplative in this sense. The Declaration of Independence asserts that we are entitled to "life, liberty and the pursuit of happiness." However, such pursuit is usually focused outward, toward personal goals, meaningful contributions to society, and enduring relationships, rather than to inner peace and happiness.

Faith in Contemplation versus Faith in Action

In a culture where looking inward is the norm, faith in contemplative practices is actively permeating the collective psyche. A few months ago, I was seated next to a Thai woman on a flight from Boston to Phoenix. We chatted, and she told me that she had grown up in a small village in Thailand. I asked what it was like being raised in her culture and whether she meditated. She said she did not meditate regularly but that meditation and a contemplative attitude were ubiquitous where she'd grown up. Like everyone, she had learned that happiness is not dependent on external conditions or possessions. As an illustration of her assertion, she related the story of a man in her home village who sold small cakes on a particular street corner. Content in his position, he represented the fourth generation in his family who had maintained the same business on the same corner for over a century. One could find his meager existence a sad lot in life, she continued, or instead, one of profound acceptance and peace.

My fellow passenger went on to explain that when she was a child, monks came to her village seeking alms every morning. She said, "The moment I put food in a monk's bowl with my tiny hand, the gesture felt so pure and powerful." Her own father became a monk for six months, as was the custom in her village, which was also a rich teaching for her. She smiled radiantly as she concluded, "Because of these things, meditation is always with me. It is in my bones. Even when I close my eyes for a moment and notice the breath, the mind gets still, and I am immediately filled with faith and joy."

This attitude toward contemplation represents a profound cultural difference that has not been fully appreciated in the West. Yet the difference is understandable. Buddhist psychology and practice have been in Western culture not for twenty-six hundred years but for less than one hundred. Perhaps if I had been raised with a culturally engrained confidence in mindfulness practices and their fruits, simple meditation instructions would have sufficed, and I would not be constantly assaulted by boredom and frustration when meditating.

In contrast, our Western paradigm seeks happiness through personal agency, independence, self-efficacy, self-enhancement, willpower, achievement, and measurable success. There are countless self-help books that encourage accepting oneself unconditionally, but such views are not supported by cultural norms. These "don't worry, be happy" messages may seem quaint and comforting in the short run, but putting them into practice is another matter.

As a therapist, I often hear a poignant and deeply engrained narrative from my clients who insist, "I can create the life I want and achieve happiness *only after* I have overcome obstacles to success, such as procrastination, fear, doubt, and unworthiness." I try to help them recognize and soften the relentless pressure residing in such beliefs, but in Western culture, this is a steep path.

Faith in Mindfulness versus Faith in Thinking

In the West we are conditioned to think rationally. My father used to tease, "Use your head for something besides a hat rack." Organized, logical, analytic thinking and the ability to sort, synthesize, induce, and deduce form the foundation of Western scholarship and education. Intuition is valued, but primarily in people who have already mastered those more cognitive skills. Einstein's renowned intuition comes to mind. For the rest of us, intuition is viewed as a first cousin to daydreaming, and we had best get on with the prevailing program of clear and productive thought. Descartes's dictum—"I think, therefore I am"—continues to undergird this paradigm.

Even within this focus on rationality, our culture has contradictory attitudes about cognition. On the one hand, we are attached to and proud of clear, rational thought. On the other, we often get caught up in obsessive, usually negative, thinking. Such largely irrational rumination can be exhausting and demoralizing. Certainly it does not lead to inner peace.

The Eastern paradigm of cognition does not espouse a love/hate relationship with thought. The mind in Buddhist psychology is considered to be a sixth sense organ. However, overreliance upon thinking is not seen as very helpful in the pursuit of happiness or freedom. Inner contemplation and mindfulness are viewed as central to that. Meditation training ultimately involves staying attentive to the flow of changing experience, and thoughts are not given special status in the field of awareness. In fact, getting overly involved with the content of thought is detrimental to the cultivation of mindfulness and therefore discouraged.

Given the cultural differences in views of contemplation, it is surprising that meditation has made significant inroads in the West. Many of us wondered whether it would be another New Age, passing cultural epiphenomenon. How could something thrive here that doesn't prioritize thinking?

The most well-known Western definition of *mindfulness* was originally put forth by Jon Kabat-Zinn, who created the mindfulness-based stress-reduction program: "paying attention, in a particular way, on purpose, in the present moment, and non-judgmentally."[2] What is this "particular way"? Although this is not specified, I believe it means holding one's attention on one object after another without conceptual elaboration.

However, most of us don't know what it means to be present without conceptual elaboration. Our association to this might be to those moments when we are absorbed in something and lose a sense of ourselves. This is not mindfulness, however, which always includes awareness of what is happening. And given our lack of understanding and familiarity with this mode of attending, we can't have much faith that being present without thinking could lead to something beneficial, much less transformative.

The results of this confusion are predictable. When Westerners attempt to practice mindfulness, our efforts are dominated by a cognitive approach. We are determined to figure out meditation, to solve the problem of "awakening." We have solved other challenging puzzles, and this is next on our agenda. Unfortunately, we are using a tool that doesn't fit the task at hand.

Paradoxically, most beginning meditators hold an unexamined assumption that discursive thinking will diminish as meditation deepens. However, because thinking is a part of our wiring, thoughts will not completely stop as we progress in meditation, any more than sounds or physical sensations will disappear. This simple misunderstanding creates internal conflict for most Westerners attempting to practice mindfulness.

The Transitory Self versus the Glorified Self

In Buddhist psychology, which is an elaboration of an Eastern worldview, the self—like thought—is seen as functional and important in negotiating the world, but if taken too seriously, it contributes to mental suffering. The self is not reified and therefore not glorified as it often is in the West. In meditation, as the sense of self is investigated, it is seen as transitory and continuously constructed moment to moment. It is to be held lightly. It is not a thing, but an ongoing process.

This supposition can be threatening to the Western psyche, which views the self as sacrosanct. It is valued, encouraged, enhanced. Self-esteem and individuation are considered hallmarks of mental health. How can this attitude that the self is less important than we thought be beneficial? Why would we sign up for that? This is another inherent area of conflict for Western practitioners.

The Patient Mind versus the Hurried Mind

The Dalai Lama once said, "You Westerners are in such a hurry for transformation. Maybe a little change every decade is enough." Eastern cultures appreciate the complexity of practicing meditation. Attunement to the inner landscape of the mind takes time and can't be hurried. It is like learning a new language.

Effective mindfulness involves cultivating and strengthening qualities of mind and heart, and, considering our long history of habit and conditioning, these must be developed gradually. I remember thinking how easy driving a car looked when I was a boy. Just get behind the wheel and step on the gas! I was unaware of the number of items that needed to be checked before getting into motion. As we shall see, mindfulness practice is similar. It is critical to understand the complexity of its workings before beginning to practice. Otherwise, we will never attain the alignment necessary for getting our meditative vehicle smoothly moving down the road.

This is no different from the training involved in becoming an accomplished musician. No one expects to be a proficient violinist after attending a weekend music camp. We understand that learning to play an instrument well takes many baby steps, much practice and patience. However, we don't recognize the analogous pace in meditation. Our expectations, woefully out of sync with reality, lead to frustration and failure when, after attending a short meditation retreat, we are not accomplished meditators, having not succeeded in leaving behind our troubles. Failing to attain the unrealistic goals we set for ourselves, we add insult to injury by sternly evaluating our performance.

Balanced Energy versus Striving Energy

Striving is pandemic in our culture. My doctoral research revealed that across the board—independent of gender, profession, or age—every subject I interviewed began meditation practice with a *striving* orientation. Each held a predominant expectation that with sufficient effort and willpower, certain thoughts, feelings, and unwanted aspects of personality would go away and stay away. This push to achieve affected me, too. I harshly criticized myself for failing to meet wildly unrealistic goals, vowed to do better next time, and became irritable and despondent. This misunderstanding and unconscious striving run deep in the West, but they are terribly counterproductive in meditation.

Steady, balanced energy is foundational to meditation. Kalu Rinpoche, a famous Tibetan teacher of the last century, expressed this perspective, one which is so difficult for us to embody:

> We can never understand the nature of the mind through intense effort, but only by relaxing, just as breaking a wild horse requires that one approach it gently and treat it kindly rather than running after it and trying to use force. So do not try to catch hold of the nature of the mind, just leave it like it is.[3]

Eventually, the subjects of my research study discovered that striving had to give way to acceptance. The transition from one to the other, however, was stressful. It was only after painstaking and often painful approaches to practice over many years that subjects were able to begrudgingly shift their way of meditating. Even then, this was done with a partial sense of resignation for most participants.

Self-Acceptance versus Self-Doubt

It seems that self-doubt and feelings of unworthiness represent greater obstacles for Western meditators than for those in the East. The Dalai Lama, representing the Tibetan tradition, and Mahasi Sayadaw, from Burma, expressed surprise at this Western pitfall, which they had not encountered in students in their cultures. Tara Brach, a psychologist and meditation teacher, called this predominant Western disposition "the trance of unworthiness."[4] As a psychotherapist I can attest to its prevalence. I can also speak to the obstacle it presents in meditation practice.

On the one hand, we are an externally oriented society, valuing action rather than contemplation, attached to thinking as our primary way of meaning-making, invested in the enhancement of the self, wanting quick results to be accomplished through striving, with a miasma of unworthiness woven through the psyche. On the other, mindfulness instructions and teaching arose in a culture internally oriented, valuing contemplation over action, viewing mindfulness as more central than thinking, less invested in self-development, emphasizing gradual development in meditation, with a psychological underpinning of fundamental worthiness.

TABLE 1: DIFFERENCES AT A GLANCE

EAST	WEST
Inward Orientation	Outward Orientation
Faith in Contemplation	Faith in Action
Faith in Mindfulness	Faith in Thinking
Transitory Self	Glorified Self
Patient Mind	Hurried Mind
Balanced Energy	Striving Energy
Self-Acceptance	Self-Doubt

Is it any wonder that meditation is challenging for Westerners? For mindfulness practices to become more deeply rooted in Western society, the differences in inclination and disposition must be addressed early on in mindfulness teaching and in the instructions themselves.

Of course, there have been some radical changes in the approach to teaching meditation over the past thirty years. Students are rarely hit with sticks when they slouch or fall asleep. Teachers, having encountered the prevalence of unworthiness in students' experiences, are beginning to make adjustments. Compassion practices, which were offered as an afterthought in teaching retreats in the seventies and eighties, are now introduced more frequently. However, the strong allegiance to traditional forms ensures that change happens slowly. Meditation teachers are still learning how to make meditation practices more accessible to the Western mind-set.

In the following chapters, I offer a variety of techniques that helped transform my own meditation practice and that of my clients and students. Early in the sixties, the side of cereal boxes offered "serving suggestions," accompanied by a picture of a smiling housewife. A typical suggestion might be "Try adding one quarter cup of blueberries and one half cup of milk!" This was followed by the disappointing realization that blueberries and milk were of course not included in the box.

The "serving suggestions" for meditation practice in the following chapters *do* include the enriching ingredients. Try adding them to your meditation practice. See how each feels. To come truly alive, meditation must not only make sense, but *feel* enlivening.

QUESTIONS FOR CONSIDERATION

Can you say more about the usefulness of the cultural comparisons you've offered in this chapter?

It is important not to idealize here or overly polarize "East versus West." Identifying general trends, however, may contribute to an understanding of why meditation might be more challenging for many of us in our present cultural context. I felt more compassion for my own struggles when I explored these differences, and it is my hope that you will feel similarly validated after reading this chapter.

You mention that the underpinning of faith in contemplation is weaker in the West. Is faith really that important? I thought the Buddha emphasized using one's own experience as a guide.

By faith I mean a deep-seated conviction that these practices are worth cultivating, that something important can be revealed thereby, something deeply meaningful. Without that backdrop, which was culturally infused during the time of the Buddha and had been valued for many generations before, meditation will simply be a curiosity. If it is only a curiosity, it will not take root.

3

THE
INNER HOLDING
ENVIRONMENT

ONE OF THE ELEMENTS that ensures successful psychotherapy—a relational activity—turns out to be essential to the internal, more solitary process of meditation. And the absence of that element in meditation explains much of the struggle Westerners have when they try to meditate.

I discovered this crucial ingredient as I was reading the work of the twentieth-century psychoanalyst D. W. Winnicott. In analyzing what made therapy successful, he found that to be truly healing, the therapeutic relationship had to include the quality of attentive caring that a responsive adult has for her child. Winnicott used the phrase "holding environment" to capture this necessary, nurturing element of therapy. Today the holding environment is considered by most therapists to be essential to productive therapy.

As I worked with struggling meditators, the parallel of the holding environment to meditation became clear to me. Like therapy, meditation is inner, relational work. And while there is no therapist involved, meditators need a nurturing, attentive relationship with themselves. I now use the phrase "holding environment" in my teaching to refer to the nurturing, inner environment that is essential to meditation.

Most people can relate to this concept. Many of us have been blessed by being "held," at least to some extent, early on in life. As adults, when we feel embraced—by nature, a comforting environment, a supportive community, the loving gaze of another, the positive regard of a dear friend or mentor or psychotherapist—we feel secure, relaxed, and open. Goodness flows from this place. The heart sings when it feels not isolated but connected, not judged but deeply accepted.

Twenty years ago, a large research study was conducted to determine (at that time) which type of psychotherapy was most effective.[1] To the chagrin of many, the study revealed that the most important factor in successful outcome, across all schools of psychotherapy, was the degree of empathic attunement of the psychotherapist. The data suggested that therapists who were perceived as warm, accepting, and understanding were most effective. To use Winnicott's metaphor, positive outcome in psychotherapy strongly correlated with the creation of a nurturing holding environment.

I want to be clear that we do not always need another person to experience being held. In fact, much of this book describes the many ways we can create an internal holding environment that has the same relaxing and nurturing qualities as when we are physically held by another human being.

It is difficult to imagine being happy separate from the presence of an internal or external holding environment. When we are out of sorts or mildly depressed or anxious, it is often because we do not feel sufficiently held or nurtured. If you stop to think about it, negative feelings quickly dissipate when we do feel held, whether it be physically by another person, when near a beloved pet, or in the comfort that familiar recollections and uplifting thoughts provide. I am convinced that much mental distress is related to a relative lack of holding environments in one's life.

In the same way, effective meditation is almost impossible without the presence of an internal holding environment. When our meditation is unfocused, discouragingly locked in a compulsive stream of thought, it is because we do not feel held. Persistent negative feelings can only begin to dissipate when we are able to establish a meaningful and nurturing context for our practice. Ongoing struggles in meditation, the difficulty many have in meditating regularly, and the high dropout rate among meditators are surely related to the inability to create and sustain an inner holding environment for practice.

Every subject in my doctoral study reported that the early years of their meditation practice were characterized by striving to control the mind. Each believed that this approach would lead to some life-changing insight; instead, it led to struggle and frustration with meditation. One subject, a middle-aged, seasoned meditator, spoke about his struggle with making intense effort in meditation:

"So you kept pushing in the hope that you would have a transformative experience?"

"Right, I hoped I would break free from my neurotic tendencies and be catapulted into a place free of self-judgment and stress, maybe even get enlightened."

"How did that work out for you?"

"Well, it's so obvious now, but of course that approach was a setup. I was being really harsh and pressured—just like in the rest of my life—so the whole thing finally imploded."

"Meaning?"

"Meditation was beginning to make me more miserable, not less. One day I got enraged because my cat crawled into my lap when I was meditating. That's when I had my epiphany."

"What was that?"

"I'm doing a practice that is supposed to lead to less suffering, and I'm suffering more! Either I have to stop meditating, or I have to consider changing my way of practicing."

"And did you change your approach?"

"Well, it took a while because I'm stubborn and I didn't want to deviate from the instructions. However, I gradually started to lighten up and relax a little during meditation. I started to be more accepting, which was a major shift."

"How long did it take to make that shift in attitude steady?"

"I pushed really hard for five or six years. I almost gave up at that point, but I stumbled into this different way of practicing. I wish meditation teachers were clearer about the importance of this more accepting perspective. Then maybe I could have seen this sooner."

Zen teacher David Schneider (who is now a teacher in the Shambhala tradition) once noted the ongoing prevalence of this pattern of early striving and frustration among Western meditators:

> There is the feeling, known to all who try it, that one does not meditate very well. The actual experience of it does not compare well to one's imagination of what meditation is supposed to be, nor to descriptions—meant to be supportive—that one might read in a book. One feels a failure at it, and who needs more failure?[2]

Most meditators will smile with recognition when they read this quote. But the question remains, why is it so common among Western meditators to strive and fail? When we learn to play an instrument, for example, which is also challenging, we don't think as much in terms of striving and failing. Why is this dynamic so prominent for meditators?

Effective psychotherapy and parenting rest on a foundation of security and trust. Meditation is no different. A mother creates a trusting holding environment, and it is from this foundation that her child gains confidence and strength and gradually internalizes those qualities and begins to feel safe exploring the environment.

A therapist, through creating a similar environment of empathic attunement, helps the client to feel secure enough to make difficult changes and to become more deeply self-accepting and comfortable with intimacy.

The same is true of meditation. Beginning practitioners need to be held by meditation teachers, not only through trusted words, but also through their holding presence. While some teachers hold space in this way, many others, while seeing themselves as agents of inspiration who offer support and instruction, seem to be only partially aware of the importance of their physical presence in the meditation hall during a retreat. This might have been enough for faithful practitioners elsewhere or at another time, but most of us in the West, in this matter of interior cultivation, benefit from a more consistent holding environment. Just as clients borrow strength from the presence of the therapist and children from the nurturing parent, so too, the meditator, in the comforting presence of the teacher, finds courage to navigate difficult mind states as they arise in meditation.

Consistency is a core attribute of the holding environment. The compelling research findings on early-childhood isolation are related to this. Children who do not get early and consistent nurturing later struggle both with intimacy and self-esteem. This need for holding is obvious. Therapists do not leave during a session while the client reflects on his or her emotional struggles. This approach would not be sufficient to create the holding environment in which safety and confidence flourish. Yet this understanding of the significance of the holding environment and how it is created has not yet been widely appreciated by the meditation culture in the West.

My own experience as a meditator is unequivocal in this regard. When a teacher is composed and present in the meditation hall, my practice is steadier than when he or she is not present. The more a teacher is available, communicating confidence and security through holding the space and fully participating in the retreat, the more consistency and acceptance—and therefore depth—show up in my meditation.

However, the holding environment created by the teacher, as helpful as it is, is not sufficient to deal with striving and frustration. The meditator, who most of the time will practice away from a teacher, needs to learn how to create an *inner* nurturing landscape.

Without previous experience and clear guidance, Westerners frequently resort to strategies similar to those reported by another subject in my study: "I tried to figure it out, control the mind, eliminate distractions and unwanted thoughts, and suppress my feelings. It was unforgiving and forced."

Most failed experiences with meditation stem from the absence of a comfortable, safe, and engaging inner holding environment for the heart and mind. Think about your own experience with meditation. When it's not flowing, isn't it because the process does not feel enlivening or nurturing? Isn't that why it's a struggle to practice meditation on a regular basis?

Because a secure, warm internal holding environment is foundational to meditation practice, this is where meditation instruction needs to focus first and foremost. When meditation teachers guide students in how to cultivate the inner atmosphere—the holding environment for meditation—then meditation practice can begin to flower.

How can a meditator create an internal holding environment when a teacher is not present? Is it possible to consciously arouse feelings that will change the atmosphere of meditation? In Buddhist psychology, strengthening positive affect is not only possible but encouraged. For example, there are practices designed to elicit compassion for oneself. In the past several years, teaching compassion and loving-kindness meditations has become increasingly common in meditation instruction to address the harsh and critical voices that can dominate the practices of students. This trend is encouraging, and early on I thought this alone might establish the holding environment essential for meditation. However, over the years I have found that to be insufficient. Compassion, and especially self-compassion, can be difficult to arouse in a climate of unworthiness, which is pandemic in the West. Part of the fabric of unworthiness, and the catch-22 of these practices, is the sense that one does not deserve to feel compassion for oneself; one is not worthy of it. Repeating the traditional phrases, "May I be happy, may I be peaceful, may I be free from suffering," simply reinforces this dilemma. One can end up swimming in self-doubt, wondering why one is not feeling any warmth at all. I have seen many students struggle with compassion meditation in this way.

So I continued my search for a single exercise that would create an inner holding environment. Then one day in meditation, I recalled touring the cockpit of a jumbo jet with my brother-in-law, who was a pilot for a major airline. I remembered looking around in amazement at the incredible array of buttons, switches, flashing lights, levers, and pedals. Watching me, David said, "It's not so simple, this business of taking off. It's not a matter of pushing one button or pedal; it requires going through an extensive checklist in a particular sequence."

A light went on in that moment, and I realized that the same might be true of cultivating an inner holding environment for meditation. It would involve breaking the process down into a manageable sequence of practices that would eventually lead to meditative liftoff. With that insight, I began to consider that not just one, but a number of qualities contribute to an inner holding environment.

Over the following years, I have identified several core qualities—the buttons, switches, levers, and pedals—that together can create the holding environment for meditation. In the following chapters, we will explore these essential cornerstones of the inner holding environment and the exercises designed to elicit them.

QUESTIONS FOR CONSIDERATION

It seems that we are always encouraged to create some kind of "container" in meditation. What is different about creating a holding environment?

It is a matter of degree. I thought I was creating a container in meditation just by bringing a bit of settling intention to the sensations of the breath at the beginning of a session. But there was no deep settling or relaxing, and I was only giving this beginning phase of practice nominal lip service. There is little appreciation in the West for the importance of creating a welcoming, comfortable, heartfelt foundation for meditation. That will not happen with a few token breaths. It is a training unto itself.

If I keep coming back to the breath again and again, and the attention stays more and more, isn't that a holding environment?

Think of the last time you were fully engaged and deeply moved by someone or something in nature. Is that how it is for you when the attention begins to stay with the breath? For most of us, that is certainly not the case. And when you *are* fully engaged in this way, do you have to bring your attention back again and again to the present moment? Doesn't it naturally stay in the vicinity? That is the point, and the function, of cultivating this type of holding environment in meditation.

4

MAKING
MEDITATION
PERSONAL

I RECENTLY SPOKE to a piano teacher who worked with children and asked him what he found most important in teaching beginners. He said a first secret was allowing them to *choose* the songs they played. Second, he encouraged them to *explore,* noodle around, on the keyboard early on.

I see "choose the songs" and "noodle around" as an equally important metaphor to engaging with meditation successfully, particularly as beginners. In fact, the first step in creating the holding environment is giving ourselves permission to meditate in a personally creative and meaningful way, rather than force ourselves to align with traditional instructions.

Traditional mindfulness instructions put little emphasis on the development and enhancement of individual needs. There is a notion in meditation circles that it's problematic to want anything from meditation, which has been called "spiritual materialism." I believe it's time to set that notion aside. It simply gives meditators one more reason to feel they are doing the practice incorrectly or to blame themselves for being selfish. Our emotional needs matter. This is our North Star. We want to know how meditation can help improve our balance of mind, increase our focus, and decrease our stress.

The Dalai Lama has emphasized repeatedly that the purpose of life is happiness. We are *wired* to be happy. It's a biological imperative. That means we are learning meditation to get happier. The sooner we adopt and internalize this basic, core intention, the better. I want fewer disturbing thoughts, more peace, more self-worth. Perhaps I include the wish that others may benefit from the work I do in meditation, and perhaps I have had direct experience with this. If I accept myself more fully, for example, I may be less likely to judge others. If I quiet down regularly in formal practice, I may be able to access this more easily in daily interactions. However, whether we are beginners or long-term practitioners, our core agenda centers around happiness.

Once we accept this reality, we can comfortably locate our own particular reasons for meditating, identifying clearly what we hope to get from the practice. Next we can tailor meditation practice to suit our goals and personality style and give ourselves permission to be creative in meditation practice, to experiment, to explore.

Memory Highlights

The assumption underlying traditional instruction is that wise and compassionate qualities of heart and mind will arise spontaneously in the course of meditation practice. Follow the basic instructions, and those qualities will develop. However, being a run-of-the-mill, restless, tense, striving, self-critical Westerner, I have not found this to be the case.

My favorite book as a child was *The Arabian Nights*. I loved the magic-on-command feature; rub a lamp and the wish-granting genie appears. Sadly, though, the famous command "Open, Sesame!" doesn't work in meditation. Ordering thoughts to disappear or tensions to ease through verbal suggestion carries no magic that creates a nourishing internal holding environment.

What can help, on the other hand, is evoking selective memories. One day, I was trying very hard to relax in meditation and kept telling myself to "lighten up." Tired and frustrated, my mind eventually drifted to a summer vacation scene from my childhood. I was lying face-down on a dock, the warm sun on my back, looking through the slats at fish lazily swimming just beneath the surface of the water. I let myself just enjoy this memory. Without any effort, my mind became relaxed and soft. I instinctively and intuitively lightened up.

The next time I found myself straining in meditation, I consciously brought that scene to mind and rested there until my mental and physical energy felt more balanced, softened. Voilà! What I had been unable to accomplish through willpower happened effortlessly through accessing a salient memory. This soothing, powerful childhood scene became the starting point for creating my inner holding environment.

I worked with James, a client meditator who, like most of us, had trouble relaxing in meditation. He came to me having tried popular guided imagery exercises offered in self-help books: "I tried focusing on healing rays of the sun, lying in a mountain pasture, basking in warm Caribbean water. Nothing! Worse than that, I got more tense because I couldn't do it."

His homework was to explore childhood memories and associations, in search of an image from his personal repertoire that would be supportive of relaxation.

The next week he came in smiling:

> You won't believe this, Doc. When I was a kid, I watched a lot of sports on TV with my dad. We always watched *Wide World of Sports,* and every year they had the cliff-diving competition in Mexico. These guys would do swan dives from a hundred-foot cliff! This may sound crazy, but I remember I used to feel a sudden sense of calm as they jumped from the cliff. I tried recalling that moment in meditation, and it worked. I brought to mind the image of the diver jumping right as I was beginning to exhale. I exhaled

as the diver jumped and experienced a sense of deep relief and quiet as the diver went into free fall. In a single exhale, I relaxed dramatically.

This would probably not be found in the top one hundred suggestions for inducing relaxation, but it worked for James. The usual approaches to overcoming difficulties in meditation differ greatly from the one I initially stumbled upon. Traditionally, five mind states are considered obstacles in meditation practice: greed, aversion, dullness, restlessness, and doubt. The three solutions typically offered for these afflictive emotions are (1) bringing direct attention to the difficult mind state, (2) reflecting on someone inspiring, like the Buddha, and (3) refocusing on the primary object of meditation, usually the breath.

For new meditators, focusing on the difficult mind state itself is challenging. Most of us don't come to meditation to spend more time getting intimate with our afflictive emotions. When one tries this approach, it will be met with resistance. Let's say I am restless in meditation. I notice the presence of tension in the body and racing thoughts. These feel very uncomfortable. I want to get away from this discomfort, which I do by spacing out in a fantasy or an irritated rant. Then I come back to the present and judge myself for being an incompetent meditator. I notice that. This process quickly degenerates, and my restlessness grows worse. Why would I want to do this? It would be like asking a new client in psychotherapy to immediately talk about something extremely emotionally distressing. We may get there after establishing a ground of safety and trust, but not in the first session. Yet this approach of "just stay with whatever arises, including unpleasant sensations or moods or mind states" is a common mindfulness instruction.

The second solution—reflecting on someone inspiring— usually yields mixed results. I may feel inspired by thinking about the Buddha or Mother Theresa, but I am also aware of how distant my own state of being—filled with restlessness and doubt—is from the object of inspiration. Now I'm feeling discouragement on top of my restlessness.

The third approach—making a greater effort to return to the focus of meditation—is often ineffective because the primary object of meditation is frequently not compelling. It is a neutral object at best. We need first to establish something positive in the field of awareness, an object that the mind *wants* to alight upon.

Experienced meditators might say that knowing that one is uncomfortable is the starting point of meditation. Before we can go further, we need to stew in our juices, recognizing how stressful it is in there. Isn't this the first noble truth the Buddha taught? "No pain, no gain" may be useful in the gym, but not in meditation. Working with difficult mind states is ultimately important, but in my experience this is more productive for Westerners *after* the inner holding environment has been established with confidence.

Most people are not interested in consciously and quietly being present to feelings such as irritation and anger and sadness, not to mention the subtle stressors of the mind. They want meditation to bring comfort and relief from emotional storms and obsessions.

Here again is a parallel to the process of psychotherapy. People come seeking relief from symptoms. In order for healing to happen, the symptoms and their causes need to be explored, but only after the client feels safety, comfort, and trust in the process. The creation of the holding environment is the first critical step, and it is equally important in meditation practice.

Before we can consciously hold difficult mind states without discomfort or restlessness, we have to learn to self-soothe, to create an internal condition of comfort and ease. Whatever our motivation for practice, the starting point is getting comfortable and confident as quickly as possible. We need positive reinforcement that will encourage us to sustain meditation practice.

I faithfully attempted to follow traditional meditation instructions for twenty-five years before I gave myself permission to explore memory in the service of cultivating the holding environment in meditation. I encourage you to try this, in your own way, in the guided meditations that follow in the next several chapters.

Many people object at first that they don't visualize well. The problem is often that they have no relationship with whatever they are asked to visualize. I was encouraged to visualize a Tibetan deity called Green Tara by one of my early teachers. I understood that she represents awakened qualities of mind to which I aspired, but I had no *personal connection* to her. On the other hand, I can easily visualize my grandmother's face in fine detail at any moment. Not only that, but when I bring grandma's face to my mind's eye, I am filled with gratitude, an essential ingredient of the holding environment. I encourage practitioners to uncover personally meaningful images from their own wellspring of poignant memories.

It takes some practice to call forth these distilled, empowering memories. Most of us are skilled at accessing unpleasant memory lowlights with ease. Memories of disappointment, betrayal, regret, and unrequited love arise regularly, not only in meditation, but in daily life. Neuroscientists have assured us that we are not alone in this, that it's universal, a byproduct of evolution. They have named it the *negativity bias.*

We are wired for both survival and happiness, but survival takes precedence in the evolutionary hierarchy of needs. When we are not mindful, which is much of the time, the mind looks for trouble, both in the past and in the imagined future. This relatively primitive troubleshooting is the reason the wandering mind is correlated with unhappiness. It may have served an evolutionary purpose, but the universal side effect is neurotic obsession and worry.

> Distraction is the only thing that consoles us for our miseries,
> and yet it is itself the greatest of our miseries.
> —Blaise Pascal

When balanced mindfulness is present, however, the negativity bias is disengaged, and this is when we have the capacity to develop new neural pathways, more conscious and less self-defeating mental patterns. In order to do this, we need the aid of a supportive inner milieu.

Distraction, worry, and obsession are frequent visitors, and they will show up when we are first inclining our minds toward positive memories. There is an art to this, and it takes some patience. For example, I can recall my exuberant first dog, Whitey, and feel a wave of delight, until I recall that his exuberance was, at times, excessive: like the time the laundry man walked into the house without knocking and Whitey bit him in the leg, which led to Whitey being taken away from me, which leads me to consider other unhappy experiences in my life, and down the rabbit hole I go . . .

There is an art to arousing positive memories and staying with the positive aspect of the memory. The initial instruction is to settle back and allow memories to come forward. This is easier said than done, because it flies in the face of our tendency to grab the steering wheel, in this case by actively sorting through the cabinet of memories. Settling back is an acquired skill in meditation. It requires a different kind of orientation, less about effort in the usual sense and more about inclining the mind in a particular direction. It is definitely not about straining. I enjoyed playing with a crystal-ball toy in my childhood. Shake it up and your fortune, or the answer to your very important question, would float up to the surface. The emphasis in accessing fruitful memories is on allowing images to float up to the surface.

One of the first things to become aware of in meditation practice is the difference between going *out* to an experience versus letting experience come to *you*.

Try this simple experiment:

1. If there is some ambient sound in your vicinity, bring your attention to it for a moment.
2. Notice that you can attend to it in an *active* way, going out to the sound, or in a *receptive* manner, receiving the sound.

3. Try this with eyes closed, moving back and forth between these two positions a few times.

Next try this with seeing. Observe how the mind can go out to see or settle back and receive the visual field. We can focus on something in the visual field or have a soft gaze as we look at the sky. Play with these modes of seeing.

This time try it with a memory. After closing your eyes, actively look for a pleasant memory from childhood. Next settle back and allow an uplifting memory to float up. Take some time with this. Sometimes surprising fragments arise, ones that you had long forgotten. At times a series of images arise, either slowly or in quick succession. What follows is a personal example:

When I was a young boy, just learning to swim, my father would play a game with me in the lake. He would stand with his legs spread wide in about five feet of water, and I would dive down, hold my breath, and swim between his legs without touching them. Then I would move farther away and try again; how long could I hold my breath? This was a powerful bonding moment with my dad.

The face of my grandmother and swimming with my father are two of the core distilled memories that often bubbled up for me during the memory slideshow. These people were my primary caregivers, so the memories themselves became the holding-environment memories of my childhood. Naturally they help cultivate the holding environment in my meditation.

In working with others, I have always found that with patience, memories like these rise to the surface, even for those who had difficult childhoods. One client, Sandra, had a challenging early environment and initially had trouble recalling any memories before the age of seven. She believed that all memories before this time were bleak and didn't want to consider another possibility. Changing the subject, I asked Sandra about her early school years. She reported that school wasn't great, but it got her out of her house, which was a relief. Suddenly she paused, surprised:

I totally forgot about my first-grade teacher. Maybe she knew about my home situation. Anyway she had these big, warm eyes, and when she looked at me, I felt so cared for. I was so hungry for that. Once I was up at the pencil sharpener, and when I turned to go back to my seat, she looked directly at me. It felt so warm and supportive that I stood there, transfixed.

This turned out to be an important distilled memory for Sandra, one we used to deepen her meditative holding environment.

My discovery of a more inviting way to enter meditation includes first learning the art of feeling good intentionally, in the present moment. We need to feel enlivened early in meditation in order to want to stay with it. Mindfulness needs to feel refreshing to ensure the future practice of mindfulness. If we are as unhappy in meditation as we are at other times, except being more aware of the unhappiness, where is the incentive to continue?

In my experience, the most reliable way to introduce safety, comfort, and trust in meditation is by evoking memories that *elicit* the feelings needed to create the foundation for our practice. Trying to *think* our way into feeling good is futile. Relaxation is one of the most fundamental aspects of the internal holding environment. We will next explore how to access a calm, relaxed state.

QUESTIONS FOR CONSIDERATION

I thought that being mindful is learning to be with what is in the present moment; are you suggesting that we distract ourselves from reality in the here and now?

Temporarily, yes. The Buddha himself emphasized the importance of creating a worthy vessel for navigating the stormy seas of the mind. Is creating the vessel a distraction? No, it's preparation for the journey ahead. In fact, you wouldn't want to leave home without it; you will be thrashing among the waves.

What is the difference between guided imagery exercises in psychotherapy and how you are using imagery with mindfulness?

Guided imagery can be used to effect positive changes in life. Here it is employed to create and enrich the inner holding environment for meditation. Once the positive feeling associated with the image arises, the memory has served its purpose, and the encouragement is to let go of the image.

PART TWO

CULTIVATING
THE HOLDING
ENVIRONMENT

I understood immediately that certain things—
attention, great energy, total concentration, tenderness, risk, beauty—were elements of poetry. And
I understood that these elements did not grow as
grass grows from a seed, naturally and unstoppably,
but rather were somehow gathered and discovered
by the poet, and placed inside the poem.

—Mary Oliver

5

RELAXATION

IT IS COMMON TO DIMINISH THE IMPORTANCE of relaxation in meditation circles; it is often seen as hedonistic, an escapist search for pleasant sensation. *Real* meditation should not be about making oneself more comfortable, but rather freeing oneself from attachment and emotional entanglement. If relaxation happens to arise as a byproduct of meditation, fine, but it should not be sought after.

I subscribed to this perspective for many years, believing that relaxation (and any form of ease-seeking, for that matter) was a sign of laziness or indulgence and fundamentally "meditation lite." After all, the Buddha wasn't interested in getting comfortable. Or was he? Didn't he prescribe a path that leads to increasing contentment and peace of mind? And isn't relaxation a central aspect of this?

In many contemplative traditions, an uneasy tension exists between pleasure and the search for deeper meaning. Implicit in the archetypal spiritual journey is the notion that carnal pleasures must be sacrificed if wisdom is to arise. Without such sacrifice, deeper insights will not be gained. Even if the spirit is willing, the flesh is weak and must be kept in check. During the main meal of the day at the Trappist monastery where I lived for six months, a brother always stood in the front of the dining hall and read scripture. The abbot told me that this was "to keep our focus on God and not get lost in the sensual world of taste."

This separation of spirit and flesh was also manifest in the time of the Buddha. Ascetic practices were the rule of the spiritual day, and eating as little as possible was encouraged. The Buddha engaged in these practices fully, and ultimately his body became emaciated, and his practice, listless. Finally, he began to question the premise of extreme renunciation:

> But with this racking practice of austerities I haven't attained any superior human state, any distinction in knowledge or vision worthy of the noble ones. Could there be another path to Awakening? I thought: "So why am I afraid of that pleasure that has nothing to do with sensuality, nothing to do with unskillful mental qualities?" I thought: "I am no longer afraid of that pleasure that has nothing to do with sensuality, nothing to do with unskillful mental qualities, but that pleasure is not easy to achieve with a body so extremely emaciated. Suppose I were to take some solid food: some rice & porridge." So I took some solid food: some rice & porridge.[1]

This was not well received by the five monks who attended to the Buddha. "[They] were disgusted and left me, thinking, 'Gotama the contemplative is living luxuriously. He has abandoned his exertion and is backsliding into abundance.'"

However, this was an important turning point in the Buddha's journey, leading to his discovery of the "middle path" between asceticism and indulgence. Part of the Buddha's insight was the distinction between the overly indulgent pleasure connected with sensuality and the wholesome sense of contentment that arises when the mind is calm and balanced. He found the latter to be increasingly important in his journey toward awakening.

I embraced renunciation during the first twenty-five years of practicing meditation, though this only became clear to me in retrospect. At the time, when I was twenty, it seemed appropriate for me to be hit with a stick; surely I could make more effort and relinquish all things comforting. During this period I fasted regularly, once going two weeks with no food or juice, drinking water only. I saw this as a way to strengthen my resolve and weaken my attachments to material pursuits. The primary form of denial in my practice during these years was a renunciation of comfort in any form during meditation itself. I simply made too much effort. I strained. This was a time when working hard was encouraged in meditation. There was far less support from teachers to soften or relax. It was "sit down and pay attention." All things come to those who strive. I embraced that motto in my practice.

Needless to say, a holding environment includes none of this mind-over-matter mode of practicing. The notion of bootstrapping ourselves with willpower in meditation will always backfire. If we are not comfortable in meditation, if there is no sense of ease in the atmosphere of our practice, if it is not refreshing, it is not likely to last. As the Buddha discovered, the pursuit of truth in a climate of denial or tension won't bear much fruit.

We humans—wired to be vigilant, scanning for threats, anticipating catastrophe, engaging in fight and flight—habitually push and pull and steer and orchestrate our experience. This leads to mental and physical tightening, a psychophysical clenching. Further straining is not helpful whatsoever to address this predicament. Yet this is what so many of us do in meditation. We just keep pushing and pulling. Have you ever played with a Chinese finger trap? It is only through relaxing that you can remove your fingers. So it is with meditation.

Relaxing the body is therefore neither indulgent nor peripheral, but the starting point in developing a nurturing holding environment for meditation. The colloquial saying "Just relax" assumes that this is an easily achievable state. It is not. In the West it is high art and takes practice, as does learning to play an instrument. We don't come home from a music lesson and say, "I failed today." Whether we have played an instrument or not, we are familiar with the learning curve involved in a new mind-body activity. Think of learning to ride a bicycle. It wasn't so easy at first, right? I remember the fateful day when the training wheels first came off. I received a loving push across our yard. Headed for one of those T-shaped clothesline poles that graced every backyard, I froze, unable to change directions, and crashed. Was that a failure or part of the learning curve?

Let's give ourselves a break and reframe meditation as a creative step-by-step process. We are learning something entirely new, a skill that goes against the grain of our conditioning. It involves less effortful attention than in the early days when we were tossed into the deep end of the pool: Pay attention! Plop down! Instead, let's start more simply, in the wading pool of relaxation.

Relaxing the Body

There are two steps in practicing relaxation of the body. I recommend that you take three to four minutes for each step, after first reading the following instructions.

STEP 1: SETTLING THE BODY

SHAKING LOOSE

Helping the body to relax is step one. This is the foundation, yet rarely is it attended to. How can a content mind inhabit a tense body? Many animals can recover very quickly from even traumatic episodes, literally shaking them off. While we do not have that capability, releasing some of our gross, physical tension is possible and strongly recommended.

There are a number of ways to relax the body, many of them familiar from yoga, tai chi, and qigong. The method doesn't have to be fancy or time-consuming; a little stretching will do.

In the first grade we stood and swayed as we sang this little song:

> Bend and stretch,
> Reach for the stars,
> Here comes Jupiter,
> There goes Mars.

I still do this from time to time; it never fails to bring a smile.

A simple method is to stand and shake out your arms and legs. Loosen all your joints. Do a few neck rolls. Sway from side to side. The form doesn't matter. What does matter is getting the body a bit looser and more pliable.

Remember the technique that appealed to you most, so you can return to it in the future.

TAKING YOUR SEAT

I am not an advocate of the straight-as-a-statue posture for meditation. Nothing in nature is that straight. You want to be reasonably upright but also at ease. As you are settling into your posture, try lifting and lowering the shoulders (almost as if they were attached to two threads, gently guiding them higher and slowly releasing), making fists for a few seconds, opening your mouth wide for a moment or two, or slowly nodding your head yes and shaking it no. These are places where tension is commonly carried, and such movements introduce a complementary response of relaxation. Just before closing my eyes, I often scrunch up my face—pursing the lips and drawing the muscles of the face toward the nose—for a few seconds. This not only helps the facial muscles to relax, but brings a childlike sensibility into the moment.

Your Breath in Meditation

Have you seen the deep, natural rise and fall of a baby's belly when he or she is breathing? We begin to lose that at around age two. Early on in life, we learn to constrict and control our breath if we feel unsafe. It's part of our defense system. It's also a way to shut down uncomfortable emotions.

The breath is sometimes seen as the gateway between mind and body. As such, it deserves special attention. Relaxing the breath allows feelings to arise and flow. An essential part of the holding environment in meditation is to reawaken the baby's deeply relaxing style of breathing.

Intentionally relaxing or manipulating the breath was, and still is, generally considered to be the province of yoga and *pranayama*. The typical mindfulness instruction is "bring attention to the flow of sensations of the breath without controlling it in any way." Because the breath has been conditioned to be constricted and shallow, that's what I will notice if I follow this instruction. Since that doesn't feel good, I am not going to want to do it for very long, or with interest. Big problem here. This is one of the initial core instructions, and following it is said to lead to important things. Not so in my experience.

Ironically, in the core teaching on mindfulness of breathing, the Buddha himself recommends calming the breath. Somehow this has not found its way with conviction into many meditation instructions in the West.

STEP 2: RELAXING THE BREATH

When we tense a muscle group and then stop tensing, there is a spontaneous response of relaxation. This is the operating principle of progressive muscle relaxation, and it is the surest way to introduce relaxation of breath also. Here are three suggestions for bringing this quality of ease into the breathing process.

HOLDING THE BREATH

Close your eyes. Enjoy an attitude of curiosity about the following process. Take three deeper-than-usual breaths. Hold the third one until some tension begins to build, but not too much. Then allow the breath to flow out. Don't push it out. Notice what happens as the breath begins to establish equilibrium.

CONTROLLED DEEP BREATHING

Holding the breath, even for a short time, is uncomfortable for some practitioners. Here is an alternative to the exercise above:

1. Take a few long, even breaths, roughly an eight count in and an eight count out.
2. Draw the breath all the way in, and push it all the way out.
3. After five or six cycles, stop on the full inhale, and let the breath tumble out and begin to rebalance your breathing.

TENSING ARMS WITH CONTROLLED DEEP BREATHING

This exercise is for relaxing both body and breath very quickly. It is effective whenever restlessness or sluggishness is present.

1. Stretch both arms out to the sides with the thumbs pointing up.

2. Take long, even breaths, roughly an eight count in and an eight count out.
3. Notice the tension begin to arise in the arms.
4. Continue until the tension increases a bit.
5. After the last full inhalation, quickly drop the arms, and allow the breath to tumble out.
6. Notice the relaxation in both the body and breath.

KEEPING THE BREATH RELAXED

In the exercise that follows, when relaxation begins to arise, encourage the breath to *stay* relaxed. This does not mean making effort that might create tension. It is more like settling back and watching over the breath in a kindly manner. When tension begins to creep back in, begin to explore ways of encouraging the relaxed breath. Perhaps tightening the breath again for just a few seconds and then letting go can reintroduce that quality of ease.

GUIDED RELAXATION USING IMAGERY

Another way to invite relaxation involves the use of imagery. Below is the guided meditation I most frequently use with clients at the beginning of a session. The intention here is to orient in the direction of ease, not to achieve perfect relaxation. We want to avoid creating a pass/fail project in every aspect of meditation, including creating the holding environment. Remember: relax as much as you can, without judgment.

1. Close the eyes, and imagine letting the weight of the body settle more deeply, giving in to the downward pull of gravity.
2. Take two or three deeper-than-usual breaths. As you

exhale, imagine tension and stress leaving the body, knots of tension melting as the energy moves down.

3. Allow the breath to establish a smooth, easy rhythm as the body continues to relax and the energy moves down in your body—as if you were safely drifting beneath the surface waves of turbulent thoughts and feelings of your mind, to a quieter and deeper place.

4. You are watching over this settling process in a kind, caring way, keeping the breath soft. You can look up at the surface and observe the thoughts and feelings above, but they do not disturb you.

5. As you become more relaxed, you may begin to notice a pleasant, contented feeling begin to arise. Slowly this feeling begins to spread, to radiate throughout the body and mind, and you are watching over this and enjoying the good feeling. It feels as if you are light, floating, effortlessly beginning to rise once again, up and up. Soon you will come to the surface, bringing the relaxed and spacious feeling with you.

6. As you approach the surface, let go of the imagery, sitting and breathing in this atmosphere of comfort and ease. Take a few more easy breaths before slowly opening your eyes.

In practicing this method of relaxing, feel free to explore your own imagery to find what is most powerful for you. I find water imagery and the downward flow of energy to be particularly effective in evoking relaxation. Nature scenes involving mountain trails and meadows have been helpful to some of my clients. One person found it relaxing to be going down into the earth in an elevator; another imagines lying in warm sunlight, soaking in the healing rays.

By watching the process as you do it, your attention stays engaged in a mindful posture. This prevents you from becoming lost in the imagery; being aware of what is happening as it is happening is a hallmark of mindfulness.

The purpose of visualizing is to evoke a particular mind-body state—in this case, comfort and ease—as we create the holding environment for our meditation practice. As the feeling becomes stable we can gradually let go of the "training wheels" of imagery.

The next element of the holding environment is playfulness. I was always delighted when creating an oceanside sandbox, building a castle with a moat, safe from the waves. Let's get into a mindful sandbox together.

QUESTIONS FOR CONSIDERATION

Is it possible to get too relaxed?

Yes, though this is not typical for Western meditators. More common is the tendency to make too much effort, followed by the counterbalance of getting sleepy. The mind gets tired of pushing, finds it uncomfortable, and tries to find release through drifting or dreaming. Mindful relaxation is an oxymoron in our culture and in our meditation. If we are mindful, this is generally occurring with effort. When we are "relaxed," most commonly we are spaced out or distracted.

My attention is sharper when I make effort, but soon this leads to tension and irritation. But when I invite more relaxation, I just drift a lot and can't seem to get motivated to arouse energy. How do I find a middle ground here?

This is a common pendulum swing. Either we make effort to focus and get things done, or we collapse in front of the TV. We alternate between hyperarousal and exhaustion. The same polarity shows up naturally in meditation practice. I have found memory imagery very helpful in finding a middle ground between these extremes and supportive of balancing energy and relaxation. A spirit of playfulness also helps; that is what we will explore together next.

6

PLAYFULNESS
AND DELIGHT

RECENTLY I WAS WATCHING MY SIX-YEAR-OLD NIECE play on the beach, running toward the water when a wave receded and running back toward me howling when the next wave crashed on the shore. Her sheer delight was palpable and infectious, and I was fully present, riveted on what was happening. In this moment of clarity, I closed my eyes and wondered why this sense of vibrancy and joy was not somehow encouraged in meditation instructions.

Not long after the beach experience, I had occasion to ask a colleague why he struggled to meditate regularly. He said, "Because it's not fun—that's why!"

Even though we all claim to understand the importance of play to our well-being, somewhere along the way our inner playful child gets lost in the shuffle. A sense of play is certainly absent in meditation, which in my view is a major cause of frustrating, uninspired practice.

Playfulness and its accompanying sense of delight are vital qualities of the inner holding environment needed for meditation. Our cultural inclination is to be overly serious about most things, including meditation. Meditation instructions can conjure up the imagined need for serious, brow-furrowing effort, with a sense that there is an ideal or "right" way to practice. They often include directions such as "focus the attention," "bring the mind back," "label," "dis-identify," "concentrate," "tame the mind," "overcome obstacles," "establish moment-to-moment attention without censorship." These words of guidance are dry and uninviting for most people, and those such as "sit still" and "pay attention" dredge up unhappy home or schoolroom memories. "Sit still, pay attention, and eat your green vegetables," my mother would admonish. (Soggy green vegetables from a can with added sugar and dye. Tasty.) A less familiar definition of "pay" may be appropriate in this context: "to seal the deck seams of a wooden ship with tar to prevent leakage." Perhaps we are sealing the deck of our minds with mindfulness in order to prevent leaking thoughts! In any case, it sounds like a sobering enterprise. I am convinced that negative associations are stirred up for many Westerners by the taming-and-controlling emphasis in many classic meditation instructions.

Participating in any activity that is foreign but supposedly good for us is reminiscent of having to take that really bad-tasting cough medicine as a kid. I still remember the time I had strep throat and the disgusting taste of liquid antibiotics. My mother's reassurance, "That's OK; it's good for you," just didn't fly. I needed something sweet.

Relaxation and delight add a spoonful of sugar, a sense of comfort and sweetness to the inner milieu. I suggest putting these first in meditation, rather than viewing them as mere by-products that may arise later in our practice. We want to feel good as soon as possible. This is the best possible enticement for learning and continuing with meditation.

The Buddha encouraged this spoonful-of-sugar approach by introducing calming concentration practices to his students. These stabilizing techniques were clearly prerequisites for mindfulness practices, leading to deeper understanding and insight. There are many descriptions of the sweetness, the *sukha,* of concentrated states of mind and how they are more deeply satisfying than sensory pleasures.

Westerners have trouble accessing *sukha* in this classic manner, because it takes us hundreds of hours of formal practice in a retreat environment to begin to access these states. We can, however, with far less practice and some creativity, begin to consciously experience some degree of relaxation and delight without external support. Learning how to create a sense of lighthearted ease within a few minutes can be a simple act of self-care in meditation.

D. W. Winnicott, who introduced us to the notion of the holding environment, saw play as a central aspect of the healing relationship: "Psychotherapy takes place in the overlap of two areas of playing, that of the patient and that of the therapist. Psychotherapy has to do with two people playing together."[1] In much the same way, meditation is concerned with a healing relationship with oneself, and inner play is essential to that.

We know the enlivening potential of play, but somehow in adulthood it is separated from the serious business of living, the same realm in which meditation itself has been cordoned off. Meditation can be promising and even profound without being "serious business." We have enough of that in our lives, which is another reason we don't meditate. Wouldn't it be a relief to know that not only is it acceptable to bring play into meditation, but that it is essential? Playfulness is an integral part of the internal holding environment for meditation. No skipping the play step. Doesn't that already make meditation more inviting?

To facilitate this, we will again utilize the process of accessing memories explained in chapter 4. Because it is difficult to arouse playfulness or delight if mind and body are tense, we first establish a basis of relaxation (see chapter 5). Once fully relaxed, we can follow the steps below to bring to mind a memory of sheer delight, whether from childhood or more recently.

Accessing Playfulness and Delight

A few preliminary tips about practicing the technique that follows:

1. Remember to allow yourself to feel settled, letting the breath be soothing.

2. Typically, the initial images that come to mind are not clear or steady and at times may seem random and disconnected. Remember, however, that the imagery that arrives is simply a gateway for allowing the joyful feelings associated with the memory to arise. This is what matters, not the precision of the memory or image.

3. You cannot fail at this exercise! Remember: this is a *practice*. Sometimes delight will arise; sometimes not. Often it will arise fleetingly, and you might try to get it back using control, which creates tension. Delight cannot be coerced; focus on relaxing and allowing the feelings to return or not.

PLAYFULNESS EXERCISE

1. First, establish some degree of relaxation and ease in the body and breath, as if you are sitting in a warm and comforting bath, feeling the small knots of tension dissolving, letting go, more and more, with each breath. Take your time to relax.

2. When you feel relaxed and your breath is easy, allow a memory of a happy moment to arise, one in which you were filled with delight and the energy that brings.

3. Continue to allow your breath to be natural and relaxed; stay with any flow of images and perhaps sounds associated with this memory scene.

4. As the memory unfolds, bring attention to how you *felt* during that experience. Let yourself savor the delight or joy or exuberance. Allow these feelings to spread throughout your body and mind. Let an inner smile form as you feel them.

5. As the sense of delight strengthens, let go of the imagery, sitting and breathing in this atmosphere of playful ease and relaxation that has been created. If tension creeps in or the

mind gets carried off in a thought stream, simply return again to the flow of imagery of this uplifting scene.
6. When you are ready, return to a normal waking state, continuing to enjoy the feelings.

We are drawn to feeling relaxed and lighthearted. If we elicit these core qualities at the beginning of meditation practice, meditation will become a less intense, more upbeat part of our repertoire.

Ambivalence about Joy

Part of learning a new skill set involves looking at the cultural and personal messages that might interfere with the practice. These early conditionings need to be understood and set aside, or they will be roadblocks to the unfolding of the practice. I have identified three major areas of potential blockage regarding playfulness and joy.

Guilt

I worked with a client, John, in cultivating joy in his meditation. One day in the office, after the guided meditation, he shared the following insight:

> The meditation is becoming very light and joyful, and I never realized that this was possible, that I could experience this much joy, that I could create it by myself. But there is a part of me that thinks I shouldn't be experiencing too much of this. It reminds me of the messages I got as a child, that somehow self-created joy is selfish.

John's experience was an example of an early internalized message around self-pleasuring, and the guilt associated with it.

Unworthiness

Often we hold a deep-seated notion that we don't deserve to be happy, that we are not worthy or will only be worthy when we have "proven" ourselves. Messages from caregivers around conditional acceptance can instill this belief. Not to mention the pressured and competitive environment we live in. Not to mention the negativity bias that keeps us more focused on the things that are *not* going well. We all have it, this thread of unworthiness running through us. Recognize the ways this shows up for you when you approach meditation practice.

Doubt

I can't tell you how many times I have heard people say, "I can't meditate."

Most of us develop skills early on in life, and we stay away from our weaknesses. In graduate school I taught a statistics class to psychology students. I was surrounded by talented thinkers and empathic clinicians who were convinced that they were no good at math. My job was to help them understand the resistance that this belief caused, so that they could open to the possibility of learning anew. I was able to offer these clinicians a corrective math experience, but only after we understood and set aside the roadblocks that they had been carrying since high school.

More recently, I worked with a client who wanted to run a five-kilometer road race, but who could not motivate himself to get to exercise even minimally. He was a somewhat overweight intellectual who had been teased in high school and told he was the "anti-athlete."

Identifying "the next step" is crucial in any journey. Having located the source of his resistance, I asked him to download a fitness app and count his steps on a daily basis. Slowly he increased the number of steps to ten thousand per day. Two years later he ran his first five-kilometer road race.

This process is applicable to eliciting qualities of mind central to the meditative holding environment. If you find it difficult to access playfulness and delight, for example, check in with yourself to see what might be keeping you from experiencing these qualities. We all have implicit rules of engagement in our families of origin. Was play discouraged in yours? Were you told that to get ahead you had to be serious? Understanding your personal obstacles further paves the way for you to have a corrective meditation experience. If you are new to meditation, doing this will help create a sense of fresh possibility. Of course you can't meditate! We are all incredibly restless and distracted by nature. This is a new training. One step at a time. Easy does it.

It might be helpful to say to yourself, in your words, something like this at the beginning of a period of meditation:

> Time to give myself a break here. I have been down on myself,
> I have self-critical voices, but I am learning something new
> and beneficial here, something worth practicing. May I take
> one step here. I could use a little refreshment in the midst of
> this busy life. Let me orient toward that during this session.

Can You Come Out and Play?

After you have noticed what your obstacles to feeling delight are, try the exercise to access playfulness and delight again, to feel the uplifting energy and the exuberance associated with the memory. Review the instructions for the exercise. Then settle back and stay open to the memory that floats up to you. Is it the same or different this time? Take it slow. This is not about getting somewhere. It is melting in place, thawing out, dropping down. Give yourself the chance, finally, to open to delight in this way. You deserve it.

QUESTIONS FOR CONSIDERATION

I get excited when I recall most early childhood playful memories, which brings even more restlessness and agitation into meditation. How can I manage that?

The good news here is that you have no trouble eliciting feeling through the use of imagery. This will be good to recall when you are struggling with sleepiness in meditation! The next step for you is to search for a memory that activates a more contented kind of quiet joy. It might be a more recent memory. The good feeling that comes from engaging in a random act of kindness may be an example. Even as we aim to elicit delight, it is important to do this in a playful, exploratory manner, until we find one or more suitable distilled memories.

One memory always leads to a train of associations for me. I hit this home run when I was a kid, and when I first envision that, I feel uplifted. But then I am thinking about how I didn't make the team the year before, because the coach wanted his son on the team, which wasn't fair because I was much better, and the feeling of uplift is replaced by irritation.

This is part of the art of using imagery in a mindfulness context. We are storied beings. No memory is an island; each is embedded in context. Practice savoring that home-run moment: the pitch, the swing of the bat, the arc of the ball, that sweet second when you realized it would not be caught. Replay it more vividly, in slow motion and vibrant colors. When distracting or upsetting thoughts arise, imagine they are floating away like bubbles. Or maybe you hit them over the fence!

7

GRATITUDE
AND WONDER

NOW THAT WE HAVE ESTABLISHED ease and delight, it's just a small step to invite spacious and tenderhearted qualities into our holding environment. Relaxation helps set the stage, and playfulness mitigates the intensity that most of us bring to meditation. Accessing a sense of gratitude and wonder further deepens the nurturing qualities of the holding environment for meditation.

Strengthening Emotional States

An important tenet of Buddhist psychology is that we can strengthen not only qualities of mind, but emotional states as well. This has far-reaching implications for our capacity to experience emotional flexibility and equipoise. In the West, few of us have been exposed to the notion that we have the ability to sculpt and shape our inner landscape. We just know that we like what we like and we don't like what we don't like. It doesn't occur to us that we can actually cultivate interest in an experi-ence that we previously found uninteresting. Or when we are irrit-ated by certain sounds, we can learn to experience these sounds as neutral or even pleasant. For example, I am writing in a library at the moment, in a supposedly silent area, and a group of people are speaking. Mild irritation led to the thought of either speaking to them directly, or to the librarian. Instead I allowed the sounds of their voices to drift into the background and experienced a moment of delight in being able to make this seamless transition in less than a minute. We tend to think that we don't have much choice about our emotional responses. They are what they are, and that's that.

What Do You Want to Strengthen?

We are what we repeatedly do.

—Aristotle

In every moment, the mind is making choices about some aspect of experience—how to react to it, whether to accept or reject it—and through those choices (carefully considered or otherwise), we continuously assign a quality of positive or negative reactivity.

This truth leads to a mindfulness principle that is both simple and profound: what we practice grows stronger, and we are always practicing, and thereby reinforcing, some mental or emotional pattern.

A natural question arises from this principle: What emotional qualities do we want to experience regularly? Agitation or contentment? Appreciation or resentment? Focus or distraction? Glass half full or half empty?

The truth of the power of practice and the choice about what we are practicing opens great possibilities for us to shape our emotional lives. However, that rests on one imperative: that we be mindful of what we are practicing. Once we have touched a hot stove, we don't want to repeat it. Similarly, when we see that (the practice of) obsessive or catastrophic thinking leads to more of the same, strengthens that habit, and encourages those tendencies to arise more frequently, we won't want to touch that stove! If we worry consistently, we will just get better at it. On the other hand, if we *practice* relaxation, lightness, and ease, those will grow in us. Although this reality is simple to understand, most of us don't act on this understanding or believe that we can do much about it. The following exercises are simple applications of this mindfulness principle.

EXERCISES: TRANSFORMING YOUR EXPERIENCE

TRANSFORMING NEGATIVE INTO POSITIVE

1. Look at something that you find unappealing. If you are in a comfortable spot, find the corner that is cluttered or unattractive.
2. Move physically closer to it.
3. Close your eyes for a moment and take three easy breaths.
4. Open your eyes and begin to notice subtle details of the object or area.
5. Reflect on the uniqueness of the object and encourage a sense of appreciation to come forward. Take your time.
6. Notice how your perspective on the object has shifted.

TRANSFORMING YOUR RESPONSE TO SOUNDS

1. Notice a sound in your environment that you find slightly annoying. It could be the hum of an air conditioner or the sound of traffic.
2. Close your eyes; take a few easy breaths.
3. Notice the subtle fluctuations within the sound.
4. Imagine that the sound is unique and has its own harmony and is worthy of your full attention.

I have often practiced transforming sound in meditation, to the point that hardly any sound in daily life is noxious to me. I now hear most sounds as unique and positive. Even a sudden loud sound or "nails on a chalkboard" now registers as neutral.

TRANSFORMING YOUR RESPONSE TO TASTE

1. Place in front of you a food item that you find mildly unsavory.
2. Look at it for a moment, and notice what goes on in your mind as you are about to put it in your mouth.
3. Put a small amount in your mouth, and close your eyes. Notice the various tastes that arise and your corresponding mental associations.
4. Imagine that this is a unique food and become curious about it, exploring the taste sensations with a sense of openness and interest.

These exercises, which transform a few aspects of our emotional experiences triggered by our senses, are not limited to meditation times. I encourage you to practice them throughout your daily life as well. Simply notice when something in your awareness is mildly unpleasant, and follow the simple steps above to perceive what is pleasant or interesting about it. As games go, this one is fun and yields great results. Through practice, you are transforming your habitual negative patterns of association. Do you remember Tinker Bell, the fairy in *Peter Pan*? When I practice these exercises, I sometimes imagine I am Tinker Bell, touching this and that with my wand, changing my perceptions and increasing my appreciation from moment to moment.

Contrary to popular opinion, our world of preferences, of likes and dislikes, is not set in stone. It is based on past experience and habitual conditioning and can be reshaped by your choice in the present moment. What has been constructed can be deconstructed. What has been conditioned can, slowly but surely, be reconditioned. This is one of the most powerful underlying principles of mindfulness, and it is good news if you take it to heart. It means that the qualities that are most fulfilling to you will grow stronger and more accessible if you practice arousing them and marinating in them. You can practice cultivating these qualities directly, without external supports. You are doing that here, as you shape the inner holding environment through practice.

> Every man carries within himself a world made up of all that he has seen and loved; and it is to this world that he returns, incessantly.
> —François-Auguste-René de Chateaubriand

In our postmillennial world, it is much more common for us to be aware of our missteps and regrets and worry, and it is to these that we return incessantly. Chateaubriand offers a good prescription however: the practice of returning to positive memories, to experiences we have "seen and loved," in this case as a way of cultivating a holding foundation for meditation practice.

Research has shown that our moods not only affect the kinds of thoughts we have, but the types of memories that get activated. Actually, thoughts, moods, and memories mutually condition one another. If I am sad, I am likely to not only have sad thoughts, but memories of past losses or disappointments, and soon my sadness deepens.

The good news, described by Chateaubriand, is that this works for positive states of mind as well. The Buddha said it this way:

> If you speak or act
> With a calm, bright mind,

Then happiness follows you,
Like a shadow that never leaves.[1]

The Buddha taught that the practice of mindfulness leads us to experience a "calm, bright mind." I propose and believe that we need remedial training—that we practice "calm" through relaxation and then "bright" through delight. These qualities, however, will not arise spontaneously; we have to be proactive in arousing them. That's what we have been practicing in the previous two chapters and will continue to develop as we move forward.

Once we have invited relaxation and delight into our inner landscape, will happiness always follow us? No, but it's a good start. The qualities of appreciation and wonder begin to add a depth dimension to your holding environment. When we think of an external holding environment, such as a beautiful place in nature or a sunset, aren't appreciation and wonder part of the experience? The following practice exercises consciously bring these same qualities into our internal milieu, in the service of meditation practice.

Combining Thoughts, Feelings, and Memories

If thoughts, feelings, and memories co-condition and support one another, let's try practicing this with the qualities of gratitude and wonder. You can begin with any of these three doorways; at some point, all three will comingle.

EXERCISE: AROUSING GRATITUDE

1. Settle back, consciously relaxing the body and breath. Allow at least three minutes for this.
2. Allow a memory to come forward, one in which gratitude

is clearly predominant. It could be something far in the past or more recent. See what comes.

3. As the images of this scene unfold, encourage the feelings of appreciation and gratitude to bloom.

4. As the feeling of gratitude fluctuates, explore what helps sustain it and what contributes to its weakening. For example, see what happens when you are totally interested and absorbed in the memory versus when you start to think about the situation itself and what it means.

5. For a couple of minutes, let go of all thoughts and images and breathe as if you were grateful for the miracle of breathing itself.

It's important to be creative here rather than formulaic. Your experience will be unique and different every time.

When doing a memory scan, thoughts and associated images often arise before feelings. In the previous exercise, I might have the thought of a lovely exchange with someone earlier in the day and then of other moments we have shared.

Within a minute or so, visual images and the sound of the person's voice may come forward, followed by the feeling of gratitude that reflecting on a good friend can engender. Once thoughts, feelings, and memories have coalesced in this holographic display, I orient more toward the feeling because that is what I am aiming to arouse.

The thoughts and memory images are secondary, in support of the feeling. When gratitude is strong, I let go of both the thoughts and images completely and sit quietly, breathing with the felt sense of appreciation. If I have practiced relaxation and delight prior to this, I will now be sitting and breathing quietly with all of these qualities present to some extent.

I often evoke the following memory of my grandmother to elicit gratitude:

My grandmother is sitting at the head of the dining room table at Thanksgiving. She looks at the children and grandchildren surrounding her. Her face conveys the deepest sense of appreciation. As I bring her countenance vividly to mind, I am flooded first with a series of images and associations about her importance in my life and then with a sense of deep gratitude. Once this feeling grows in intensity, I elicit additional grandmother memories in order to sustain the feeling of gratitude. After the feeling is somewhat stable, I let the image of her face recede, and I sit and breathe with a strong sense of appreciation.

By practicing these qualities individually, we gradually "internalize" them, learning to recognize when they are present in our internal landscape and when they are absent. As we practice, it becomes obvious to us, for example, when relaxation weakens, and we know how to invite it back in. Gradually we become more confident and skillful in managing the fluctuations in our internal world and making appropriate adjustments. At this point we are bringing three qualities—relaxation, delight, and gratitude—into the foundation of our meditation practice. You may begin to notice that in moments when all three of them are present, the overall feeling of contentment is richer than when only one or two are there.

It may seem that there is a lot going on, a lot to monitor. That's because landscaping the internal environment is relatively foreign to us. Yet, all of these qualities are present without even consciously realizing it when we are watching a sunset, for example. Eventually, this is what happens in our internal world as well.

Wonder Filled

Wonder is appreciation on a grand scale, the sense of awe that comes when we see our individual drama in a wider context, our lives against the backdrop of humanity, our planet as one of billions. For some it may arise in a stunning natural landscape. Whatever the vehicle, the sense of wonder takes us out of our neurotic preoccupations and connects us to the wider network of life. When wonder is present, we feel held in a deeper and more unconditional manner. This is why wonder is an essential part of the internal holding environment and why we want to learn how to consciously access it. Though wonder is universally appreciated when it occurs, most people don't realize they can cultivate or elicit it by choice. Consider the following for a few minutes before practicing this exercise:

AROUSING WONDER

1. Take a few minutes to settle the body and soften the breath.
2. Bring to mind a time when you felt amazed, deeply moved by the magnitude or mystery of life. Stay with this memory in a relaxed manner for a few minutes.
3. Allow the feeling of wonder to grow stronger and spread through body and mind.
4. As the feeling of awe or wonder fluctuates, notice what images and associations help to keep the feeling strong.
5. In the last couple of minutes, allow the imagery to fade, and breathe with a sense of wonder, as if it were quite amazing to be sitting and breathing and simply aware.

AROUSING MULTIPLE QUALITIES

At times, a detailed memory can evoke several of the holding qualities we are trying to cultivate. This is one I personally hold dear to my heart.

I am six years old. We are on summer vacation at a lake in Connecticut. At five thirty in the morning, I hear the sounds of my father rustling about the cottage, which is comforting. I also hear the sound of a single-engine plane flying nearby, which is soothing in my half-awake state. Smells from the kitchen arrive now, and my father is gently waking me. Quietly, I get dressed and come to the kitchen, where he and I eat in silence. Taking a flashlight, we head down the path to where the rowboat is tied to the dock. My father takes the oars and softly dips them in the water. Mist sits on the water like a cloud; the sun will rise before long. Soon we are in the vicinity of "the hole." My father fished here with his father when he was my age. He tells me that back then several boats would try to get into position in this spot because it was known as the best fishing area in the lake. This morning, we are the only boat. My father gauges our distance from shore; he calls on his own memory to locate the exact place and then lowers the anchor. We sit in bonded silence, connected with history and the mystery of the natural world, fishing for more than two hours.

This memory brings forth all of the qualities we have so far considered—relaxation, delight, gratitude, and wonder. While I recommend initially evoking one quality at a time, at some point several may come together like this in a more complex memory gestalt. It is no coincidence that the central characters in these two memories—my grandmother and my father—were my most nurturing caregivers.

You may want to explore this field of memory in your own experience. For me, it was my grandmother and father; for others, it might be a sibling, aunt, teacher, or mentor. Because wholesome caregivers may have been an essential part of our early holding environment, patiently unearthing the poignant memories involving them can support us in the development of our internal holding environment in the present.

QUESTIONS FOR CONSIDERATION

I find myself getting attached to sweet feelings when they arise, but theoretically I'm not supposed to get attached to anything, right?

This is a concept that gets many meditators in trouble. We can't stop being drawn to pleasant feelings. The Buddha struggled with this issue also, imagining that to deepen his understanding he needed to rid himself of all attachments. Finally he discovered that healthy attachment, *chanda,* is necessary, as opposed to unhealthy attachment, *tanha.* In this case we are creating the holding environment, essential for deepening meditation. It is important to welcome and encourage and appreciate positive feeling in this context. If we start to hold on too tightly, however, this leads to craving, *tanha,* which creates tension in the mind and body and thereby disrupts the holding environment. Think of appreciation versus desperate grasping.

I was taught to just be with things as they are and that insight would arise from observing experience from that vantage point. You are recommending actively changing our view of phenomena. Can you explain further the function of this?

We need to develop confidence in working with the internal landscape, seeing that we can change our perspective at will, which in turn will shift our mood. In this way we begin to understand the degree to which our reality is not found, but cocreated moment to moment. Even moods and assessments are not as fixed or solid as we may have imagined. This is both a useful training and an important, encouraging insight in mindfulness practice.

It feels like these exercises of cultivating the holding environment for my practice can be useful in daily life. I have found myself playing with them in daily life. Is this a good idea?

Definitely! I have found this to be one of the most relevant applications of mindfulness in daily activity.

8

WARMTH AND TENDERNESS

THE FINAL HEART QUALITIES to be invited into the holding environment are warmth and tenderness. We could see this as the organic unfolding of appreciation and wonder. Once these qualities have been awakened, we will naturally want to bring care and sensitivity to more of our experience.

Thanks to Tara Brach, Sharon Salzberg, Chris Germer, and others, compassion and self-compassion are increasingly important in the teaching of mindfulness to Westerners. It took a while for teachers to see how students here judged themselves consistently and harshly. Slowly this is being recognized and addressed, with more emphasis on acceptance, and specific compassion practices, from traditional Buddhist teachings, are more regularly offered.

Though I see this as a very positive development as mindfulness becomes mainstream in the West, my personal and clinical experience has been mixed in working with compassion. The usual suggestions for arousing compassion involve the mental repetition of traditional phrases, such as

> May I be happy.
> May I be peaceful.
> May I be free from danger.

Some practitioners have had success in working with these phrases. If this is so for you, wonderful! They represent a struggle for me personally, however. Even when I have worked with them over extended periods of time, they have not been effective in moving me from the mind to the heart. Worse, because no warmth has been forthcoming, additional self-judgment has arisen in this form:

> This is not surprising. Maybe you are not very compassionate anyway. The disappointing memories you have are easily accessible. Maybe that is the "bedrock" of who you are. Maybe you are avoiding this painful truth, and this is what you should be focusing on.

A traditional alternative is to first bring to mind someone who has been a beneficial presence in your life, imagining that person is sending you love in an unconditional manner. After eliciting some feeling of warmth in this way, shift the attention to yourself, and begin sending compassion within. Many of my students, as well as yours truly, get caught in an unworthiness undertow when engaging in this practice. We don't believe we are deserving recipients of the love that the beneficial other is sending. In short, we get hung up in defeating thoughts and judgments when we try to arouse self-compassion in the standard ways.

I have found it helpful to get the heart involved through a series of baby steps. There is no way I can go directly from a restless or a scattered mind to self-compassion. It just doesn't work. It's too big a leap. I get cranky and resistant. That is why I first encourage the cultivation of more accessible heart qualities in creating the inner holding environment.

In addition, the word self-compassion is loaded for many of us. Since a thread of unworthiness runs through most of us, this practice immediately bumps up against resistance. So even when it is time to address the territory of self-compassion, warmth or kindness or friendliness is easier to digest initially—after that, tenderness, if it's available.

Imagery and Tenderness

It is important at each step of this practice to understand the aim, the feeling you are trying to arouse, and then find language and imagery *suitable to you* in support of moving in this direction. Finding your own gateway into these practices keeps meditation alive.

For example, bringing to mind an image of my cat, curled up in the sunlight, awakens a warmhearted sensibility in me. You may or may not be a cat person, but we all have images in our memory catalogue that will serve the same purpose. It might be a memory or series of images of a special person in your life or the felt sense that this person is near, watching over you. At times I will imagine that a warm light is entering my body at the top of my head and slowly moving down all the way to my toes. As the light slowly moves down, my mind and body become soft and spacious.

Take it easy. Be mindful of the tendency to strive, which is the fast track toward tension, claustrophobia, and failed expectations. The heart doesn't respond well to commands or formulas. Simply wondering how to invite warmth or kindness into the atmosphere, inclining the attention in that direction, is one place to start. This moves the practice away from orchestration and willpower, and invites trust into the deeper currents of our being. We want to make an opening for creative imagination to surface.

Tenderness becomes a natural extension of warmth. Our individual experience of what tenderness feels like, of how it manifests in our life, is unique and sacred to our emotional landscape. Thinking about being more compassionate to myself is a desert, but inviting an image of myself at age six will open a stream of tenderness. A pet, a young child, a dear one who is struggling, a baby bird, a personally moving interaction—what evokes this sweetness for you?

Remember: we are practicing, learning to play a new instrument. It's not like flipping a switch. It is inner play. We are creating, step by step, an inner holding environment for meditation. The attention will never be completely steady in these practices. Awareness is jumping around constantly. Distraction is universal. We need to have a relaxed and playful attitude throughout; that's why these are the first two qualities we cultivate.

We have all experienced the state of flow or peak experience, a state where we are fully engaged and enlivened in the midst of what we are doing. It's a state we cherish and would like to experience more often. It doesn't occur to us that we can create this state internally, but that is precisely what we are practicing here. Consider the qualities we have been cultivating: relaxation, playfulness, delight, appreciation, wonder, warmth, and tenderness. Aren't these the qualities that are present in the state of flow, when you are intimately engaged with a loved one or enthralled by a luminous sunset? These same qualities are foundational in establishing a holding environment for meditation practice. Quite simply, if these qualities are not present, the mind will seek greener pastures elsewhere and will lose interest in meditation. For meditation to take hold, it must both make sense and feel good, and the "feel good" needs to show up early in the process. We do not need one more medicinal discipline or another activity in our lives based on the principle of delayed gratification.

It is possible to be mindful of an object without any feeling whatsoever. I can hold my hand two feet in front of my eyes and gaze at the palm and fingers clinically. I call this "casual" or "halfhearted" mindfulness. This is a frequent occurrence in meditation practice. It is also a central reason why the mind wanders—and why people stop meditating. Without feeling, without interest, there is nothing compelling to keep the mind in the vicinity.

Try this experiment. Hold your hand out at arm's length and look at it casually. Notice your relationship to this experience. Now cup your hands about twelve inches in front of your eyes. Carefully observe the detail of your hands as if they were wonders of nature, precious, as if you were seeing them this way for the first time. This is what I call "wholehearted" or "therapeutic" mindfulness, and it encapsulates what we are cultivating in the atmosphere for meditation. And what is wholeheartedness if not the confluence of ease, delight, wonder, and tenderness? Ultimately, we don't want to walk through our lives simply attentive and nonjudgmental. There is no juice in that. No one wants their epitaph to read, *He was more mindful more of the time.* We want vibrancy and sensitivity and gratitude. We are also more likely to meditate if it brings forth these qualities. If this is manifesting in our practice, we are likely also to be more attentive and nonjudgmental, both in meditation and in life.

Creating the Wholehearted Holding Environment

There are four areas of focus in creating a wholehearted holding environment:

- Relaxation and ease
- Playfulness and delight
- Gratitude and wonder
- Warmth and tenderness

I encourage you to spend time strengthening these qualities within your internal landscape. Pay attention to your felt experience when these feelings are present and when they are not. Notice the difference between casual attention or halfheartedness in meditation and wholeheartedness. How does each feel?

When you can summon these qualities in your meditation, this will already feel like an enlivening, restorative activity. In teaching meditation to clients, I now spend a significant period of time supporting the development of this foundation.

In my own meditation practice, I invite these qualities in this order. I also check occasionally to see if they are present as I am meditating, and if one or more is weak, I attend to it and encourage it to come forward, generally through visualization. Feel free to explore these heart qualities in different orders. Discover what is effective for you. Being a "serious" meditator, I always need to start with relaxing and then lightening things up. I recently received a message from a therapist I worked with a few years ago. She said, "It took me a while to understand the importance of playfulness in establishing the holding environment. I kept trying to go directly to compassion, in my own practice and in my work with clients. Now I see that feelings of warmth can be accessed so much more readily if we give ourselves permission to play first."

Mindfulness involves cultivating attention, but I have found it beneficial to focus upon emotional mindfulness first and foremost. Without this as a foundation, the mind will ruminate, fantasize, obsess, and analyze rather than soften and want to remain in the vicinity of the present moment. It is not until we can settle down comfortably and with interest in the present that meditation can yield additional fruit.

QUESTIONS FOR CONSIDERATION

Before I actively visualize, I need to spend a few minutes thinking about compassion and how I really want to cultivate it, even though I am a relative beginner. Is that in line with what you are suggesting?

Wise reflection was something that the Buddha encouraged, and I believe it has a place in "setting the table" for mindfulness practice. The key is to know what the intention is for your reflection, whether it is helpful, and when to stop reflecting and move more directly to imagery. Otherwise the attention can get hijacked into story land.

Light and dark are connected when I practice using imagery. I start out with something positive, but then it morphs into a negative association. How do I stop that from happening?

This is quite common. The mind tends to drift toward that which is unresolved, toward the glass half empty. It is important to see the prevalence of this self-defeating pattern. We are cultivating a new, wholesome habit here, which takes caring attention. A few words can be helpful when you notice the mind drifting toward the dark forest. At those times I might silently repeat, "You don't want to go down that rabbit hole." One of my favorites is, "You are still a good person." This quickly helps me to smile and relax, and from there it is easier to move back to positive elements of imagery.

Can you say more about "core distilled memory" images?

It sometimes takes a while for these to emerge. I work with a student who has struggled to arouse warmth in his meditation. Recently he reported that he felt a softening in the area of his chest, coupled with sadness. He stayed with that, and the image of him rocking his two-year-old child came to mind. This was followed by the image of himself as a two-year-old being rocked by his father. He did not search for these images; they came to him. He was immediately filled with tenderness. This has become a core distilled memory, and he draws upon this regularly when setting up the holding environment for his meditation.

What if I don't remember much from my childhood?

This could be another reason to judge yourself, and we don't need more of that. Sometimes memories will arise over time if we incline in that direction, sometimes not. Remember that we are not chasing images or memories; we are aiming to elicit the core feelings of the internal holding environment. The memory of my cat's antics this morning can arouse playfulness in my meditation tonight, and her consummate skill at relaxing I sometimes call to mind when I am settling down in meditation.

Is it possible to "exhaust" a core distilled memory image?

There is a natural tendency for the mind to habituate almost anything. A core mindfulness skill is that of anti-habituation, seeing things freshly, again and again. Working with these core images can occasionally get dull, but more frequently they become even richer and more textured, and the feeling associated with them becomes accessed more readily.

PART THREE

TRANQUILITY PRACTICE

Only a tranquil mind is able to hold itself
aloft in the light of contemplation.

—Pope Gregory I

9

CONCENTRATION BLUES

A FEW YEARS AGO, I had the privilege of participating in a four-month retreat with the Burmese teacher Pa-Auk, one of the foremost masters of what is called "concentration meditation," or "concentration practice." I figured that I would make progress rather quickly. After all, I had been practicing meditation for many years. However, my first few weekly interviews with him were brief and humbling. I would give a brief report of my meditations. He would then smile, cock his head, and say, "Concentration still weak." End of interview. Finally, after more than two months of following the flow of sensations of the breath at the tip of my nose, the only technique offered, I went before the master. I told him there was only the slightest wavering of attention during a three-hour period of meditation. I felt confident that he would be pleased with my report. Pa-Auk paused and smiled. He pointed to his nose, still smiling, and said, "No wavering." He looked directly at me, no longer smiling, and repeated, in a sober, sincere voice, "No wavering."

Concentration practice invariably opens a can of worms for Western practitioners. The word evokes cognitive strain and will-power, tightening and narrowing the field of attention and holding it there. I am reminded of the famous Rodin sculpture, *The Thinker:* chin on fist, brow furrowed, the essence of intense focus. For Westerners this sculpture embodies the archetype of concentration. However, such an effortful, strained approach is counterproductive for all manner of contemplative and meditation practices.

In addition, it is easy to fall into a frustrating pass/fail relationship with concentration practice. The instruction is clear and leaves no opportunity for reframing: stay with the object of attention. No other experience that arises during the practice, however marvelous it may seem, is acceptable. Pa-Auk was only interested in whether my attention stayed with the flow of sensations of the breath. Nothing else mattered. No cookies. No other measure of progress. No wavering.

Why Bother with Concentration?

Stability and calm, the underpinnings of insight, are the essential qualities cultivated in concentration practice. Stability arises when the attention can settle and focus. Until then, it is unable to gaze steadily at the workings of the mind. Without stability, one's focus is like that of a handheld video camera: the image is constantly shifting, and it is difficult to establish clear focus. We do not need this level of stability when dealing with the contents of the mind, with our stories. To look more carefully into the underlying, moment-to-moment processes at work in the mind, however, requires another level of refinement in attention.

The establishing of deep calm is equally essential. As concentration matures, the mind begins to move away from its predominant obsession with thought and begins to focus on the flow of sensory experience, most commonly the sensations of the breath as it makes contact with the nostrils. With further progress, the mind begins to rest in the flow of physical sensations. This is experienced as a great relief. A deep feeling of contentment begins to spontaneously arise when the mind is not bombarded with negative and ruminative thinking and feeling. There is a tremendous sense of freedom in this. It feels like a new discovery, an inner resource that one never knew was possible, a shelter from the storm so near at hand. One has learned to create a beautiful haven that is restful and compelling. It is a peace of mind into which difficult mind states do not intrude.

In principle, this sounds good, doesn't it? Don't we need more of this in our highly distractible, stimulus-rich culture?

Redefining Concentration

Given the clear benefits of concentration practice, perhaps we must find a more appealing yet accurate label for it. The Pali word *samadhi* has been translated as "concentration." However, *samadhi* connotes pacifying and composing the mind and carries several other meanings that are more accessible for Westerners, including "quiescence" and "tranquility." These words elicit different associations than "concentration." They are accurate yet more useful for us, given our cultural predisposition to cognitive striving and goal orientation.

While it's true that the core elements in these practices are stability and calm, putting calm first and foremost, both in understanding and practice, is much more effective for practitioners in the West. This is not just because we need much more of it, but because when the mind is first calmed, it is more likely to settle and stay. Just ask my cat. If, when she's racing around the house, I try to get her to stop first, hoping she will then calm down, she'll fight me. Once she is calm, however, then she settles down, like a heavy snow falling in a forest on a still night.

Yet that's what I tried to do for the longest time in my attempts at concentration practice. I tried to get the mind to stay, in the hope that calm would follow. Instead, what followed was frustration and self-condemnation for "wavering."

We've already learned that relaxation is the first component of the holding environment. Here, we are deepening the felt sense of calm, the physical manifestation of peace. Calm and ease are fundamental to progress in meditation, and we are culturally deficient in this territory. We bypass calm in mindfulness training at our own peril.

Tranquility in the Big Picture

To sidestep the negative word associations, I will sometimes use *tranquility* as a synonym for *concentration*. I can't say enough about training in tranquility as a distinct skill in meditation. It has numerous physical, mental, and stress-management benefits and adds a new dimension to self-care.

In the context of mindfulness training, tranquility steadies the mind, helps to make it flexible and pliable, and readies it to hold any aspect of experience up to the light, so that it may be considered with care and from a number of angles and perspectives. The Buddha was quite clear about the strong correlation between concentration practice and insight; it is a necessary prelude to wisdom. The insight and understanding that we experience in meditation is only as deep as the calm stability that undergirds it.

Our capacity to stay both present and tranquil is clearly the weakest link in the mindfulness chain for Western practitioners. William James, a psychologist and novelist who took an early interest in Buddhist contemplative practices, discovered that in his experience, it was not possible to stay focused on an object for longer than eight seconds. He was right: without tranquility training, that's about all we can manage. If we open the field of awareness without developing this skill, we will be able to stay with the process for about eight seconds before spacing out. Tops.

Given this somewhat unnerving reality, how does one develop and practice tranquility in a manner that is accessible? How does one come to inhabit this quality of presence? How can we come to embody a state of concentration with balance and ease?

QUESTIONS FOR CONSIDERATION:

I get anxious just thinking about concentration because I am so terrible at it. It feels like I can't stay focused for more than a few moments on anything!

Many times we feel alone in our practice. I would often "peek" at my fellow meditators during a retreat and think, "Everyone is getting this except for me!" When it comes to concentration, we are all in the same boat. However, we avoid or bypass this element of meditation at our own risk, as this will diminish the effectiveness and depth of our practice. The question is how to address this challenge in a meaningful fashion. Pushing harder is not the solution.

10

TRANQUILITY
GAMES

MAMMALS PLAY FOR THE DELIGHT OF IT. Human beings are no exception. This is a good thing, or we would never get off the ground with tranquility practice. The question is not whether to play or not to play. The question is what games are most helpful to arouse desired qualities of mind. Having spent years painfully grinding away at concentration and seeing others do the same, I am convinced that in order to make progress in meditation, Westerners need to tap into creative play. Otherwise, mindfulness meditation practice is doomed. When I was a kid, my friends and I would say, "You are doomed!" to each other and laugh. It still brings a smile to my face today. It's also an appropriate word to employ in this context. *Webster's* defines *doomed* as "likely to have an unfortunate and inescapable outcome; ill-fated."[1] Without engaging creative play in our meditation practice, it can be a similarly doomed and ill-fated endeavor.

So, play is important to avoid a doomed meditation practice. Before you begin to play, however, it is important to establish the intention for your meditation session.

Intention/Aspiration

Why do you practice tranquility? It's important to be clear and unequivocal about the reason. Whether it is to calm down a little, take a break from the bombardment of external stimuli, prepare the ground for open awareness and inquiry, contribute to the welfare of the planet by detoxifying your congested psyche, or take the next step toward whatever you imagine to be profound awakening, be clear and *repeat it to yourself,* either silently or out loud, with feeling.

I often do this a few times until I feel aligned with my intention. The first time or two, it may be just a ritual of halfhearted repetition. It's important to get heart and mind connected immediately by doing this wholeheartedly.

Keep your intention fresh. Don't use the same phrase or phrases each time. Make it personal and relevant, using *your* words. Why are you doing this practice? Maybe yesterday I wanted to save the world, and today I just need a break. So be it. Take stock. Be honest with yourself. Notice when you feel connected to your intention. You are establishing the mental-emotional posture for your meditation journey.

Wholehearted Engagement

Once clear about your intention, next you need to check the emotional landscape. Whatever your intention might be, even if it is to relax and unwind, affective engagement is the next important step. Without that, the mind will neither settle down nor get interested in the process of meditation and will slip into cognitive drift.

I am here to marvel.
—Goethe

Simply being more aware, more present, is necessary but not sufficient in meditation and in life. I am reminded of Mary Oliver's poignant aspiration to be "a bride married to amazement."[2] Bringing this vibrant sensibility into your meditation, in a series of small steps, is the next agenda. The heart must be invited in right at the beginning; this is an essential cornerstone of practice.

The first tranquility game has this invitation to the heart as its aim. Below is a version I often use myself.

TRANQUILITY GAME: INVITING THE HEART

The first quality to invite is calm, which is a challenge for many of us. I was often quite restless; the wild energies of my mind felt like feral horses. Many years ago I would try to overcome initial agitation with willpower. Having seen the futility of that approach, today I proceed to play a game in the service of evoking relaxation. Sometimes I include horses in my visualization:

OK, a little speedy and stressed this morning, distracted. How to settle these ponies down? I bring imagery to mind in support of this and evoke the following scene.

Maybe the horses are hungry or thirsty; let's find some water and tall grass over here in the shade of this big tree. Slow down—that's right. Drink some cool water in the shade. Easy does it.

My breath begins to slow down and become smooth in response to these words and imagery. I allow my attention to notice details of the horses, the tree, and the brook. Settling is a gradual process, and I know that trying to narrow the attention too much or limiting it to just a small patch of the scene will likely create more agitation. I stay with this until my energy level is settled significantly.

How do we quantify "significantly"? On a scale of 1 to 10, with 1 being extremely lethargic and 10 being the most agitated and restless you have ever been, what number represents your energy level at this moment? Rensis Likert, a twentieth-century psychologist, discovered that we can make this self-assessment without thinking about it and that the numbers reported correlate, more or less, with the experience of others. My 4 is relatively close to your 4 because we all know the ends of the scale, extreme lethargy and extreme restlessness.

My recommendation is that you stay with the game of settling until you are energetically in the proximity of 4. That's calm enough that you can feel relaxation in the body and relief in the mind, so that the mind is more inclined to settle down a little, but not so calm that you are drifty and dreamy: calm with backbone, not calm like mush. Without this level of settling, what follows will be a struggle. So find 4, and begin to acquire a feel for it; this is an important dimension of creating your holding environment.

I generally attempt to stay with this process for at least five minutes.

Next you want to expand the emotional connection and investment, starting with *playfulness or delight*. The intention here is to increase the energy level somewhat—move the 4 to 5. Don't let this bring restlessness or distraction back in. Instead, the uplifting quality of delight is what you are inviting.

One particular morning, I imagined I was eight years old, on the way to a baseball game with my father, feeling the anticipation of going to Fenway Park to see the Red Sox for the first time. I stayed with this memory for four minutes, until a feeling of gladness arose and comingled with calm.

Gratitude is next in the ingredients of the holding environment, and this is near at hand. I reflected on how much my father supported me in countless ways, and I only needed to allow a few precious memory snapshots to float by to access this heart quality. Three minutes.

Kindness or friendliness toward myself is next. A Polaroid snapshot of my sister and me, holding hands, all dressed up, taken on the front steps on a Sunday morning soon after a poignant loss, came into view. Sweeter now with time. Three minutes.

Wonder is the final emotional ingredient in the holding environment. I brought to mind my very first memory, of awakening in the middle of the night in my crib, hearing the heating pipes creaking, and experiencing the first sense of a separate self beginning to form. Then, at five years old, experiencing the miracle of bringing a seemingly dead shrub back to life by faithfully watering it day after day. Then the images faded, and the wonder of this breathing in the present moment and the awareness of it. Six minutes.

The mind was supple by then and bright; the breath was soft; the heart, appreciative and open. This entire meditation took twenty minutes. Time is not the important factor here. Sometimes I take more time, sometimes less: as long as it takes for calm and the heart qualities to show up in meditation. My state of mind is then settled, refreshed, enlivened. It is tranquil and engaged. Why wouldn't I want to do this again tomorrow?

A template is embedded in the above game, an order in which qualities of mind and heart are coaxed and invited. But there is room for an infinite variety of explorations, room for creative use of imagery, memory, and personal meaning making. The idea is to get the heart involved. Finding your own way to do this is crucial.

I can't say enough how important it is to simply stay with engaging the heart, no matter how long it takes. I have spent many a meditation session just on this game. Almost always, when I check in at the beginning of a meditation session, I find that I can't settle, and the heart is not available. In the old days, I just tried to force it, which led to futility and self-recrimination. No longer.

If I find myself disconnected from the heart when I sit down to meditate, I take it as an opportunity to change course and cultivate the unification of mind and heart. I reflect a bit, consider what might be useful, and then use my imagination and memory to evoke what needs to be evoked. I know there is no point in rushing it. Feeling can't be coerced, only invited. If the entire session is utilized in this way, it is time well spent. The need was acknowledged and addressed, and I can now move forward in the next part of my day in more harmony.

As we move deeper into tranquil concentration, the groundwork has been laid.

QUESTIONS FOR CONSIDERATION

There seems to be more roaming around in your approach, more permission for that. I like the idea, but I am so undisciplined that I worry I will just wander.

Knowing what we are doing and why we are doing it is critical. Yes, there is more permission, more leeway to explore and discover what is most effective. But the direction toward balanced continuity is always predominant. A frequent problem is the overemphasis upon continuity at the expense of tranquility and balance. For short periods it is possible to focus intensely in a continuous and precise manner. But this can't be sustained. This approach soon creates tension, and the organism wants to expel this endeavor as if it were a foreign object. For many meditators this leads to the misplaced notion that one needs to try harder to sustain continuity. A vicious, self-defeating cycle ensues. Excessive pressure to focus is the bane of Western meditators. The Buddha used the metaphor of tuning the strings of a lute. If they are either too tight or too loose, the instrument will not produce the desired sound. So too in meditation. It is possible to be "too loose," but this is not generally the case for Western practitioners.

There is a lot of emphasis upon setting things up properly, which requires patience. I have so little of that, and I like to push through obstacles. How should I handle that?

Appreciating small gains in the moment and taking the focus away from future, idealistic goals—these represent huge and important shifts in orientation. A famous yogi once remarked that idealism is a form of violence. That may be dramatic, but it highlights the fact that setting the bar unrealistically high keeps us from appreciating what *is* happening. This is a major and largely unrecognized contributor to dissatisfaction. We are creating meditation one small step at a time. Has anyone ever produced sweet music without first emitting a thousand squeaky sounds? Relax, smile, savor, and gradually transmute that pushy energy into a gently persevering and long-enduring mind.

11

MAKING
CONCENTRATION
ACCESSIBLE

TRADITIONAL INSTRUCTIONS for developing concentration are pithy, to say the least, and this can inadvertently fuel an internal conflict for meditators in the West. Take, for example, these paraphrased classic instructions that Pa Auk recommends:

1. *Stay with the flow of sensations of the breath at the nose tip.* Nothing here suggests that this might be challenging and that one should anticipate struggles.
2. *When the mind wanders, immediately return to the flow of sensations of the breath.*
   That's all there is. To make matters more frustrating, the immediate fruit of this practice is highlighted:
3. *Soon the mind will become calm and steady!*
   This only intensifies the dilemma, since there is nothing like this experience on the horizon for most of us. Instead, this can easily become an exhausting dualistic struggle, as the noble part of the self attempts to overthrow the impure, oppositional, laggard self. Worse, one looks around the room and imagines that everyone else is getting it and that he or she is the only failure at this practice, which increases

a sense of isolation and failure. Who wants to share this abject sense of failure with the teacher? No one wants to be in the bottom third of the class. Is it any wonder that a few seasoned meditators, struggling with a sense of incompetence and frustration, left Pa-Auk's retreat early? So we are again left with the question of what Western students of meditation need in order to avert the struggle and disappointment so prevalent here.

For deeper tranquil concentration to be accessible for Westerners, I have found the following two practices to be indispensable.

1. *Maintaining the holding environment*

   The first is the determination to create and maintain a holding environment for meditation, regardless of the instructions you receive. This involves both calming and getting affectively engaged, as explored in chapter 10. I have learned through painful trials that not settling, not getting the heart involved, leads to stress and self-doubt. The Pa-Auk retreat posed one of the greatest challenges to my newly discovered perspective because, despite moments of doubt, I did *not* stay with the instructions but met my needs for calming and inviting the heart to participate in various ways. It spared me much additional suffering.

   Please first allow yourself to settle, to trust that that is what is needed, and give yourself full permission to do that.

2. *Momentary concentration*

   Once a tranquil state has been attained and the heart aroused, momentary concentration practice encourages the attention to alight on multiple objects momentarily and sequentially. In this practice there is no one specific object or anchor for the attention. Instead, you permit it to alight on one object after another in succession. A favorite metaphor for this practice is derived from the old TV show *Sing Along with Mitch*. I was allowed to stay up past my bedtime to watch this program on Saturday nights. Mitch Miller and his barbershop quartet performed favorite tunes, and as they sang, the lyrics appeared at the bottom of the screen. The best part was that a ball of light bounced from one word to the next, so even if you didn't know the song, you could sing along with Mitch! Momentary concentration is following the bouncing ball of attention from one moment of experience to the next. This form of concentration practice is much more accessible for most Western practitioners.

Focusing on a single object is more easily attained after some proficiency has been gained in momentary concentration, which gives the mind more freedom to move around. The restless energies of the mind can roam a bit more. This is what Shunryū Suzuki Roshi, the famous Zen master, was pointing to when he suggested that the best way to tame a wild horse is to give it a wide pasture.

The challenge of momentary concentration involves learning to stay with the bouncing ball of attention and not simply wander away. Initially keeping attention in the sphere of sensation supports the mind to not drift or distract itself in the thought world. We are deeply conditioned to identify and engage with thoughts. Here it is best that we rely on physical sensations as our training ground for concentration. For this reason, I strongly encourage you to direct the attention toward sensory experience—in particular, sounds, body sensations, and visual imagery—when doing this practice, and away from thoughts and feelings.

Working with Sensation and Sound

GUIDED MEDITATION 1:
MOMENTARY CONCENTRATION WITH BREATH AND SOUNDS

1. As always, take a few minutes to settle the body and soften the breath.
2. Establish the holding environment, arousing qualities of delight, gratitude, warmth, and wonder. (These first two steps may take several minutes. Take your time.)
3. With each exhalation, imagine energy moving down, releasing with gravity.
4. Maintain relaxation of the breath, but with no particular object of focus.
5. Begin to notice some of the minute sensations of breath at the tip of the nose, in the downward flow of the exhalation, as if that flow were actually comprised of a few smaller wavelets and particles of sensation.
6. With each exhalation now, notice a few sensations as the breath passes the nostrils. What before was a flow of breath is now seen as many smaller sensations.
7. Imagine that these sensations are soothing.
8. Keeping the breath soft, begin to notice sounds on the inhalation.
9. Listen carefully and precisely. If you stay with one sound, notice that it is comprised of many smaller, fluctuating nuances of sound.
10. Imagine that the sounds are compelling, sweet.
11. Feel pleasant sensations of breath on the exhalation; listen to the harmonious sounds on the inhalation. (I sometimes imagine a lightning bug flashing in the dusk of evening, lighting up sensations of breath on the exhalation and sounds on the inhalation.)
12. Allow everything else that arises in your field of experience to remain on the periphery or in the background.

13. Keep checking to see that the breath is moving easily. When you discover that it is tense, take a short timeout and turn your attention to relaxing the breath.
14. Take a few more easy breaths before slowly opening the eyes.

Trying to attend to a single object is initially too claustrophobic for the restless minds of many Westerners. Momentary concentration gives the attention room to roam, but not too far. The parameters are clearly delineated; thoughts and feelings are not invited in at this time. We are so eager to include thoughts and feelings into mindfulness practice, because this is the territory we are familiar with. However, until concentration is quite stable, thinking will simply lead to more thinking, and that will not strengthen mindfulness. This is why momentary concentration practice, without clear parameters and guidelines regarding thinking, will be far less effective.

Gradually you will want to widen the parameters of momentary concentration. Eventually thoughts can be integrated. This needs to be done slowly and systematically, however, so that the attention will not be seduced by habitual cognitive patterns. The exercise below provides guidance for this widening.

Labeling Thoughts

To protect against being swept away, some practitioners find it useful to attach a label to the type of thought or feeling that is arising (e.g., "planning," "judging," "evaluating," "rehearsing," "fantasizing," "remembering"). This reinforces the observational posture of the mind. It is also helpful to not "sink" into a thought, even if one is labeling. Thoughts are seductive. Best to note the thought before moving quickly but gently back to breath sensations or sounds. In the following beginning exercise, you will elicit positive thoughts only.

GUIDED EXERCISE 2:
MOMENTARY CONCENTRATION WITH THOUGHTS

1. As always, as if for the first time, take a few minutes to settle the body and soften the breath.
2. Establish the holding environment, arousing qualities of delight, gratitude, warmth, and wonder.
3. With each exhalation, imagine the energy moving down, releasing with gravity.
4. Imagine the out-breath to be tumbling out, like a waterfall moving down.
5. Maintain a state of relaxation on the in-breath, with no particular object of focus.
6. On the out-breath, briefly invite one uplifting thought. Label the kind of thought you have noticed.
7. On the in-breath, notice a series of sounds (as in the previous exercise).
8. Invite one pleasant thought with its label on the exhalation, a series of sweet sounds on the inhalation.
9. Check frequently to see that the breath is flowing easily.
10. Take a few more easy breaths before slowly opening the eyes.

When you have had some success with this practice, you can try noticing two and then three thoughts on the exhalation. This is the equivalent of advancing to the next level of difficulty in a video game. You can also attend to sensations of the breath on the inhalation, instead of sounds. *What* we are attending to is not as important as the *qualities* of attention we are cultivating. In this case, we are cultivating continuity and precision in a relaxed and engaged manner.

The following analogy serves me well when working with thoughts. Have you ever flown a kite? I imagine that the kite is the thinking mind, and the string is the connecting observation, the knowing of the thought. If I let go of the string of observation, I become lost in thought, and the kite flies away or falls to the ground. As momentary concentration grows stronger, it is possible to hold the connecting string for longer periods of time.

Exploring Receptive Attention

I stumbled into the final secret ingredient for deepening concentration by accident. One day I became exhausted by making a strong effort to follow the bouncing ball of attention and decided to take a break. I went outside and lay in the grass in the warm sun. There were a few small black spots, or "floaters," on the surface of my eyes, which were highlighted by the brightness of the sun. I noticed that if I tried to hold one of the spots in my field of vision, it scurried away. But if I relaxed my attention, the spot stayed! In a sudden burst of insight, I realized that I had been leading my moment-to-moment experience, chasing it, rather than following it.

Learning to stay receptively attentive when the mind is settled is one of the high arts of meditation. Generally we are either (a) attending to something actively, (b) spaced out, or (c) absorbed in an experience. When mindfulness becomes more stable and is accompanied by relaxation and interest, a fourth mode of perceiving becomes viable. Attention can be present without effort. I had previously experienced this outwardly, when watching a sunset for example, but not in meditation. This was a revolutionary breakthrough in my practice.

There are two main postures of mind when relating to experience, most simply described as directed and receptive, or moving *toward* and opening *to*. The easiest and most accessible example is in the relationship with sound, as you experienced in an earlier meditation. You can either move out to a sound or settle back and allow the sound to wash over you. It doesn't take muscles to listen.

The capacity to stay in receptive mode increasingly in meditation is an extremely important training, and one which we may not easily stumble upon. This is not the natural inclination in our culture, which is to be more assertive, to move out and capture experience, take hold of it. Grasping has found new footholds with the deluge of social media. Constant connectivity is the new "must-have" in our culture. Because of this constant social pressure to move outward in an acquisitive manner, to make oneself visible (selfies come to mind), it takes some practice to trust that experience will come *to you,* that you don't have to create it or go out and get it. It can be quite an insight to recognize that if you settle back, experience keeps arising all on its own. After acquiring a taste for this mode of experiencing, it is also a great relief. It takes less energy. You don't have to work so hard to organize the flow of your experience. Even thoughts keep coming if you settle back! It was groundbreaking when I began to trust that I didn't have to rehearse the next thing I was going to say, in conversation or in the office, that the next appropriate phrase or gesture would arise spontaneously on its own if I stayed relaxed and present.

This can be practiced both in meditation and in daily life. You simply have to notice when you are reaching out for sound, for example, and settle back into a more receptive posture. Same sound: different mode of attending. You don't even have to close your eyes. Try it now.

Listen to a sound in the vicinity. Notice that you can reach out to it, so to speak, or receive it, simply settling into a posture of attending, as if the mind were a satellite dish receiving frequencies. One often hears that it is not the experience, but the relationship to the experience, that changes in meditation. This exercise is a concrete way of shifting one's core relationship to experience. In particular it supports a settling-back orientation, which in turn is critical for a deeper and more sustainable meditation practice. The previous two guided meditations emphasized active or directed mindfulness. The next meditation weaves *receptive mindfulness* into the practice.

GUIDED EXERCISE 3: RECEPTIVE MOMENTARY
CONCENTRATION WITH BREATH AND SOUNDS

1. As always, as if for the first time, take a few moments to settle the body and soften the breath.
2. Establish the holding environment, arousing qualities of delight, gratitude, warmth, and wonder.
3. With each exhalation, imagine the energy moving down, releasing with gravity.
4. Imagine the out-breath to be tumbling out, like a waterfall moving down.
5. Maintain a state of relaxation on the in-breath, but with no particular object of focus.
6. Notice that the breath is moving *all on its own*. Remember: as with all creatures, the body is "breathed" naturally to maintain life. Establish this receptive perspective.
7. Notice the difference between *leading* the breath, which is directed attention, and *following* the breath, which is receptive attention.
8. When the mind moves into a more directed mode of attending, notice this and return to a receptive mode of attending.
9. On the exhalation, allow sensations of the breath to come to your attention.
10. On the inhalation, allow sounds to come to your attention.
11. If the mind gets too relaxed or drifty, allow the attention to become a bit more directed. For a few breaths, on the out-breath attend to a few precise sensations of breath, and on the in-breath attend to a few precise sensations of sound.
12. Then invite a more receptive quality of attending once again.
13. Play with these alternating modes of attending to experience and see how they weave together. Emphasize receptive attending, but invite directed attention when the attention becomes too lax.

14. See if you can move from directed to receptive modes of attention, and vice versa, without becoming distracted.
15. Take a few more easy breaths before slowly opening the eyes.

Traditionally, *verified faith*—the direct confirmation in one's immediate experience that meditation is effective and beneficial—creates positive reinforcement in one's practice. This is to be distinguished from *taking* something on faith, the assumption that it must be so because an esteemed other, or the Internet, says so. Approaching mindfulness practice, we may have provisional faith in the Buddhist teachings or the research studies on mindfulness or the teacher we are working with. Verified faith, however, is said to arise when benefits, such as calm and steadiness, begin to show up directly in one's mindfulness practice. In this case, I may theoretically understand the value of tranquility, but I move to verified faith when I taste tranquility and experience its benefits. Because of some combination of lack of interest, striving, and agitation, however, these encouraging qualities do not arise readily for many Westerners, so conceptual faith does not straightforwardly graduate to verified faith.

These step-by-step exercises—maintaining the holding environment, developing momentary concentration, and inviting receptive mindfulness—are the keys to making progress in tranquil concentration and the gateway to verified faith.

QUESTIONS FOR CONSIDERATION

I was taught that this kind of momentary concentration was "insight" practice. Can you say more about the difference between concentration and insight practice?

Insight is not something that can be practiced per se. It is a fruit of practice. We can only create the conditions from which insight may arise. One of these core conditions is tranquility. Various insights will arise, at different levels, in every form of mindfulness practice. Not all of them are delightful. The first insight is that we are much less present than we thought! This is followed by insights into how wild and uncooperative the mind is at times, how it doesn't respond to our bidding or willpower. This is why, when practicing concentration, it is so important to have previously introduced lightness and warmth into the holding environment. With balanced practice and inquiry, further insights arise into the causes and conditions, the inner moves necessary for positive qualities of heart and mind to arise more frequently. Following this are insights into the nature of the mind, the radical impermanence of experience, the ways we create unnecessary trouble for ourselves, and how to substantially mitigate that. These insights arise and deepen in the fertile soil of calm, heartfelt, steady attention. Often we focus too much on acquiring the insight fruits and reaching for those in unbalanced ways. Instead the intention here is on creating the conditions in which the plant can grow and mature, trusting that fruit will happen as a result of kindly and dedicated tending.

Active versus receptive mindfulness is a new concept for me. Does this require self-monitoring during meditation, or is this something that will arise on its own?

Because we tend to "lean into" meditation practice, because we are so oriented to steering, leading, controlling, and orchestrating, both outside and inside, because this is the water we swim in, I have found it particularly helpful to bring special attention to this tendency and to consciously invite receptive attention. We need to see how predominant active attention is in our orientation and the limits of that approach. It can be a genuine surprise to see that the world does not fall apart if I stop directing attention and to discover the richness of receptive mindfulness, which takes less effort and more attunement. Again, this is an acquired taste, one that requires practice and trust. If I take my hands off the wheel, there is less control about what arises in my experience, which could be unsettling at first. Starting out simply, with sound, is the simplest entrée into this exploration.

12

DEEPENING
TRANQUILITY

EVEN AFTER PRACTICING concentration meditation for some time, we mustn't put our toys away and get too "serious." When mind and heart have arrived and settled, when the attention is more inclined to be present (because the grass is quite green here and now), there are still a number of ways to enrich the experience. There are four dimensions that can further broaden and deepen tranquility: calming, saturating, spreading, and stabilizing. There are games— creative meditation exercises—for each.

MEDITATION EXERCISE: DEEPENING CALM

The challenge as calm develops is to stay connected to the experience, to stay aware of what is going on. This is the one area where we can let the lute strings become too slack. When we are lying on a beach for example, the mind is generally lost in thought or dreamy meandering. What we are aiming for in this exercise is a deep sense of serenity without losing the awareness that watches over and protects it. In the previous chapter, we identified 4 as the ideal number on the Likert relaxation scale for cultivating the inner holding environment for meditation. Here we are leaning toward 2.

This is a delicate training because as relaxation deepens it is natural to begin to drift in a trancelike manner and become lost in the experience. This is why images that evoke both grounding and ease are best. Floating in warm Caribbean water, for example, may be *too* relaxing.

However, the image of lying on fragrant grass on a warm spring day with pleasant sounds can work. This image captures elements of soothing and grounding simultaneously.

In the following sequence of tranquility exercises, the starting point builds on what we have cultivated in the previous chapter. As we move along, these exercises are nested within one another. Before beginning, be sure you have settled considerably and invited the heart qualities of delight, gratitude, warmth, and wonder, so that the holding environment for your meditation has been established to some degree.

MEDITATION EXERCISE: CALMING

1. Imagine that you are lying in a field of fragrant grass next to the ocean. The temperature is comfortable; the rays of the sun, warm and soothing.
2. With each in-breath you smell the fragrant grass.
3. With each out-breath you feel the warmth of the sun.
4. The rhythmic sound of the ocean also holds you.
5. The pleasant feeling that accompanies this calm is compelling; you are naturally drawn to it.
6. With each breath more calm arises, and you move ever closer to the calmest state you have ever experienced.
7. Enjoy this state for a few minutes.
8. Imagine that the warmth of the sun and sound of the ocean are now gently energizing, circulating warmth throughout your body and mind.

9. Take a few more restorative breaths before slowly opening the eyes.

MEDITATION EXERCISE: SATURATING

Saturating connotes soaking completely through, the way steady rain gently soaks the soil in your garden. In this exercise, tranquility saturates every corner of the body, heart, and mind; no part is left out. It is as if there is one undifferentiated blanket of tranquil attention covering the landscape. As always, establish the holding environment for this exercise before proceeding.

1. Imagine that you are lying in a field of fragrant grass. The temperature is comfortable; the rays of the sun, warm and soothing.
2. With each in-breath you smell the fragrant grass.
3. The smell fills you, permeates every cell of the body, soaks into the mind, and saturates the atmosphere.
4. With each out-breath you feel the warmth of the sun soaking deeply into all the cells of your body, with no cell left out. The warmth is all-consuming, inside and outside.
5. Saturated alternately, rhythmically, by the fragrant smell of the grass and healing warmth of the sun, you are drawn toward a state of contentment as compelling as you have ever experienced.
6. Enjoy this state for a few minutes.
7. Imagine that the warmth of the sun and fragrant smell of grass are now gently energizing, circulating warmth throughout the body and mind.
8. Take a few more restorative breaths before slowly opening the eyes.

MEDITATION EXERCISE: SPREADING

This exercise addresses the expansive quality of attention, which moves outward in an inclusive fashion and in every direction. As water in a reflecting pool occupies every square inch of space, so tranquil concentration spreads completely and fills both inner and outer landscapes. Inside and outside become less distinguishable. Consciousness extends throughout to the edges of the landscape and beyond.

Take the time to create the holding environment for meditation, and then continue with this exercise.

1. Imagine sitting in a warm tub of water.
2. The tissues and cells of your body begin to unwind, succumbing to the soothing warmth.
3. The mind also begins to release its tension and agitation.
4. The edges of the body, the boundary between inside and outside, begin to dissolve in this soothing warmth.
5. A profound feeling of warm contentment begins to move outward, as if filling the entire room.
6. Now it seems to spread beyond the edges of the room in every direction, boundless.
7. Enjoy this state for a few minutes.
8. Imagine that a warm energy begins to now radiate through the body and mind.
9. Take a few more restorative breaths before slowly opening the eyes.

MEDITATION EXERCISE: STABILIZING

While stability is traditionally considered the hallmark of concentration practice and the main quality to be cultivated, I see it as the unfolding of the water lily arising in the wake of calm, spreading and saturating. As these qualities mature, a deeply rooted settling and firming of attention begin to manifest. This is classically referred to as "one-pointedness." Now we can allow attention to begin to abide, to rest, on a single object. As always, create the holding environment for meditation again before doing this exercise.

1. Imagine you are a mountain, solid and settled.
2. Imagine the weather changing in various and dramatic ways, while you remain settled throughout.
3. Imagine the temperature fluctuating, but you remain settled.
4. Imagine variations of light, but you remain settled.
5. Conditions change constantly, but the qualities of solidness and settledness endure.
6. A profound feeling of contentment begins to arise in the body and mind.
7. Allow the attention to settle on the feeling of contentment itself.
8. Rest comfortably in this feeling. Savor it.
9. Imagine warm energy circulating throughout the body and mind.
10. Take a few more restorative breaths before slowly opening the eyes.

These exercises can be done individually or sequentially, developing and enhancing one dimension of tranquility after another. Spend time on this aspect of practice. Come to enjoy it. It is rich and valuable in its own right.

This practice also prepares you for deeper understanding and insight. We are drawn to deep comfort and ease, but we are also "meaning-making" beings, creatures who by our very natures are hardwired to search for truth, to better understand the workings of our mind, and to find purpose in the world we inhabit.

QUESTIONS FOR CONSIDERATION

When I try these exercises, there is more inclination to drift, to err on the side of wandering mind. I struggle with that because staying present at all costs has been a core guiding principle of mine for a long time.

Staying present is not only the implicit instruction of mindfulness instructions, but the explicit one. There is no argument that presence is the cornerstone of mindfulness. It's the second half of the way you express it—"at all costs"—that is complicated. In my experience, *striving* to be present, as if that were the only tool in the toolbox, has created unnecessary suffering. The issue at hand is how to encourage and develop a natural willingness to be present, to find new and engaging ways to do that. First we have to see how tightly we have been holding the steering wheel, to look directly at how it feels to do that, and to give ourselves permission to relax this tight grip. On a very basic level, there is no way to develop continuity of attention when we are holding and controlling tightly. Mindfulness can only be present in short bursts in this context, and all too often these periods alternate with periods of exhaustion and discouragement. In deepening tranquility, inevitably there are periods when the mind meanders or fantasizes. However, this is an improvement over obsessional rants and self-critical tirades! Gradually the mind begins to find a deeper, quieter place of balance, ease, and presence. It is a lovely surprise when the mind returns on its own to the calm holding environment, without having to be coerced in the slightest, simply because it is the greenest pasture.

Is it possible to get too calm and concentrated? I heard that if we are not careful, it is possible to get overly attached to deep states of concentration.

I have heard this caution voiced by teachers and read about it in the texts, but I have never experienced it or spoken to anyone who struggled with this problem in the West. That would be a good problem for most of us to be dealing with. The more prevalent issue is too little concentration, too little calm, and too little emphasis upon developing it. It is possible to fall into a sinking, dreamy state when doing these practices, which can be sweet, but where mindfulness is rather weak. Part of the balancing act here is to check to see whether there is an observing/holding quality of mind present, knowing what is happening as it is happening, not letting go of the kite string of attention. There can be attachment to the soporific reverie and an unwillingness to bring more mindfulness into the equation for fear that the sweetness will dissipate, but that is not too much concentration; it is too little mindfulness. This needs to be monitored.

PART FOUR

THE
CULTIVATION
OF INSIGHT

The real voyage of discovery consists not in seeking
new landscapes but in having new eyes.

—Marcel Proust

13

THE SEVEN
FACTORS OF
OPTIMAL PRESENCE

I ONCE HAD A TRANSFORMATIVE EXPERIENCE in a very ordinary setting. I was sitting near the edge of the ocean, drinking a bottle of fruit juice, distracted. A bee buzzed closer and landed on the edge of the bottle. My first impulse was to swat the intruder away. Suddenly I was transfixed: the elegant, colorful hovering of the bee, the sunlight twinkling on the bottle, the soothing sound of the waves lapping the shore, a heart-piercing sense of harmony and belonging rippling through my nervous system, flooding my senses. Everything appeared mysterious and precious. Disparate sounds became harmonious, resonant. I felt fully alive, an energized participant-observer who began to experience everything in this light. Sights were vivid; sounds were magical. Even the bee alighting on my bottle of juice, the bee I had considered swatting in irritation and fear just a moment before, had as much right to be here as I did. Realizing that I could change my entire state of mind without changing anything externally was profound. The experience led me to ask important questions, the same questions that Buddhist psychology asks regarding this state: What does the state of deep, heartfelt presence consist of? What are its component parts? How can this state be accessed more of the time?

These questions are asked within the context of the abiding truth that all of our experience, both inside and outside, is in a state of constant flux. In the West we try to control our external environment, so it is pleasant, comfortable, predictable. We try to avoid painful feelings and disquieting thoughts.

From the Buddhist vantage point, this approach may have limited, short-term efficacy, but ultimately it is limited precisely because of the unreliable, constantly shifting nature of *all* experience. This turns everything on its head. What can be done if nothing is stable? This is the ultimate existential challenge of Buddhist psychology. Recognizing this flux as the fundamental backdrop of experience, the challenge becomes how to find contentment in this erratic landscape. According to the Buddha, the key to deeper satisfaction is to be found in the cultivation of specific qualities of mind and heart, rather than in favorably manipulating elements of the external environment.

When first practicing meditation, I was under the impression that mindfulness was the *only* important mental training and that all good things would follow from that discipline. Many years later I learned that there were classically *seven* factors involved in optimal presence. These qualities are present when the mind is deeply engaged and focused in meditation but also when we are fully engaged and connected in any life situation. They arise when we are doing something we love or are surrounded by natural beauty or are listening intently. They are present when I am sitting by the edge of a lake, imagining that everything before me is exquisite.

Classical Arrangement of Factors of Optimal Presence

Below are the qualities of optimal presence in the order in which they are said to classically arise in meditation practice:

Mindfulness: The capacities to be aware of what we are experiencing in the present and to remember to return to the present are the central qualities of *sati,* or mindfulness. This quality of mind is central and necessary but not sufficient for full presence.

Investigation: In this context, investigation means to closely observe all of the sensory and mental experiences in the present moment. It does not include analyzing, reflecting, comparing, synthesizing, figuring things out, or intellectualizing. It is not the investigation of the *content* of experience, but rather of the underlying processes, such as the changing nature of phenomena and the cause-and-effect links in experience. This focus of investigation is completely foreign to our cultural context, in which content is king and in which we identify so completely with our world of thoughts and stories. We will explore this factor in depth in subsequent chapters.

Energy: The Pali word *viriya,* or energy, means a steady and balanced effort, in the 4 to 6 range discussed in chapter 11.

Joy: Delight arises when the mind is steady and engaged in the present moment without strain. The Buddha spoke of this as non-sensory joy, because it arises without external props. This brings a sense of accomplishment as the wild energies of the mind become harnessed. This type of joy can be more satisfying than sensual pleasure, providing powerful positive feedback for sustaining meditation.

Calm: Gradually the mind and heart move toward a more subtle level of contentment, which is less thrilling but more peaceful.

Concentration: Joy and calm are the precursors to concentration. Now a natural stabilization arises because the mind wants to settle, because it is both delightful and calm in the present moment.

Equanimity: The mind is balanced and views phenomena impartially, neither holding on to experiences nor pushing them away. Everything begins to arise with evenhanded acceptance.

Rationale for This Order

The order of these factors was discovered long ago through the consistent reports of early practitioners. *Mindfulness* naturally leads to keen *investigation* of the ways the mind works, especially with respect to the creation of mental suffering. The Buddha was clear about this. He did not advocate paying attention randomly, but encouraged looking into suffering and its causes. He was a physician treating mental suffering.

As it starts to become clear how mental suffering was being created—primarily through overly identifying with aspects of experience that are impermanent—*energy* is naturally aroused. Why? The meditator begins to see something he or she has not previously understood—that there is a clear, available path to reducing mental suffering. Contrary to our prevailing wiring and conditioning, it is *not* about getting rid of unwanted thoughts and feelings. Rather, the secret to reducing mental suffering is consciously settling in a balanced, accepting manner into the flow of experience. This results naturally in the meditator being more invested in this mode of caring attention. He or she can now exercise agency in the process of reducing dis-ease and increasing well-being.

The discovery that one can reduce one's own suffering leads to *joy*. The attention becomes rapt, the mind less interested in spacing out or seeking greener pastures elsewhere. There is an element of slight restlessness and excitement in this joy, and over time the mind settles into an even deeper contentment or *calm*. In turn, this state of calm ultimately opens the path to a steady, riveted attention, or *concentration*. The final factor of *equanimity* allows or invites whatever arises in experience in an evenhanded manner, while maintaining the previous six factors of presence.

A New Template for Western Meditators

This classical order does not translate straightforwardly for Westerners. Because of our restlessness and strong attachment to discursive thought, the traditional unfolding of these factors of presence is stymied.

Mindfulness—the intention to bring our focus into the present moment—is the cross-cultural starting point. Whereas in the East this naturally leads to an investigation of the processes of the mind, in this culture it often leads to thinking, which can lead to more thinking, a proliferation of cognitive problem solving and analytical, psychological types of investigation.

Because of this overarching tendency to figure things out, mindfulness does not readily link up with an investigation into the causes of mental suffering and what can be done about it. Therefore balanced energy will not come forward. If energy is not properly aroused, then joy, calm, concentration, and equanimity have little chance of showing up in a stable fashion. In short, the meditator is left with a great deal of wavering, and the practice is destined to remain a conflicted and frustrating mystery.

The following is the proposed, more effective order for many of us:

Mindfulness is the starting point, but our tense bodies and restless, thinking minds need to be addressed first, so we first cultivate mindfulness in the service of relaxing, settling, and *calm.*

We then further cultivate the holding environment, inviting more *energy,* interest, and affect, including *joy.*

Now, with positive reinforcement established in meditation and the mind naturally inclined toward the present, it becomes possible to practice *concentration/tranquility* meditation. This then becomes the platform for a balanced, inclusive *investigation* that leads to broad-based acceptance and *equanimity.*

TRADITIONAL ORDER	WESTERN ORDER
Mindfulness	Mindfulness
Investigation	Calm
Balanced Energy	Joy
Joy	Balanced Energy
Calm	Concentration
Concentration	Investigation
Equanimity	Equanimity

How to Experience This Optimal State More Frequently

Meditators eventually pose a vital question about optimal presence: how can I elicit this wholehearted state more of the time in my life?

Once we have learned to identify these qualities of presence in our meditation experience, we can check to see which of them are present and creatively invite those absent to join. This will enrich our experience, not just in meditation but in life. For example, I am walking down the street, distracted, not particularly aware of my body, and noticing my surroundings only to the extent that I don't bump into anything. Which qualities of presence are available? *None of them.* This is what I call "casual" or "halfhearted" attention, something we are all familiar with.

Suppose I stop and take a deep breath. I become aware of the body, noticing sights, sounds, smells. I imagine that everything I sense has its own unique beauty, and I imagine that I am connected to all of it. And I become aware that the ability to think and perceive in this way is a miracle. Voilà! Mindfulness, energy, joy, calm, and even concentration have come into my experience, and I am more fully engaged in heart and mind.

In time, we learn to elicit these qualities in formal meditation. And when we do, the mind is settled, pliable, and prepared to begin the journey of investigation.

QUESTIONS FOR CONSIDERATION

I was taught that just paying attention to what is going on was the main point and that everything would follow from that. Why aren't these factors emphasized more?

They are in the texts, but again, perhaps at that time and cultural context these qualities arose more spontaneously and straightforwardly. Here it is different, and in my experience the cultivation of these factors needs to be front-loaded in practice instructions. Just as there is more interest in self-compassion practices currently, stemming from our pandemic sense of unworthiness, I believe there will be an increasing wave of interest in these seven factors of awakening, as they are traditionally called.

There seems to be more self-monitoring, or evaluation of my practice, involved in your recommendations. I previously have only checked to see if mindfulness was present. Doesn't more reflection and self-monitoring lead to excessive thinking and analyzing?

Because we so regularly get hijacked by thought, there is a tendency to eliminate it almost entirely in many meditation instructions, as if thinking were the enemy. Since discursive thought is one of our central meaning-making mainstays, the pendulum has swung too far here. Using reflection and monitoring judiciously and pointedly in meditation can be extremely helpful. We are not inviting thinking randomly; we are using words that help us locate and assess the internal state they are pointing to. I ask, during meditation, "Is calm present? Is balanced energy present? Is joy present?" These are not theoretical or tangential questions. They are inviting a direct look, on the spot, at the composition of the internal landscape. If these qualities are found to be weak or absent, the next encouragement is to invite them, to be creative in inviting them. Why? Because they are the soil and water and sun of mindfulness, without which the flowers of compassion and understanding will not grow.

14

INVESTIGATION GAMES

A CLOSETED "EXPLORER" resides in each of us. We like to solve puzzles and look for buried treasures. I remember the thrill of an Easter egg hunt or a simple game of hide-and-seek. These games captivate our attention. They hold our focus as long as we have a chance of solving the puzzle or finding something special. Otherwise discouragement creeps in and we lose energy.

Effective mindful investigation benefits from harnessing this natural interest.

However, it is important to create games that are challenging but not exasperating. One of those other Western tendencies—the need to push, strive, overcome, master—can show up at any time in meditation. In the context of investigation, we can set the bar unrealistically high, fail to reach the goal, and get self-critical about our perceived sense of failure. Seeing this self-defeating pattern is itself an insight that can arise from investigation.

True investigation, in the Buddhist psychological sense, is another of the qualities said to spontaneously arise with mindfulness practice. Unfortunately, this too has rarely been my experience, not unless there are specific directives and invitations to *look in particular ways*. Our inclination to think about the content of experience and analyze it runs deep. We are content junkies. So when we begin to practice mindfulness, this type of thinking and analysis comes to visit. If there are not very specific instructions about how to identify these thought habits while inclining toward new and interesting ways of considering our inner world of experience, we can find ourselves swimming in the same old pond, and new insights will not arise.

The insights highlighted in Buddhist meditation practice are directed toward the infrastructure and processes of the mind; they are not usually involved with *content*. However, seeing the limitation of thought and the stress involved with identification with its content can be an extremely important investigation. I've realized over time that my own narcissistic preoccupation has caused me considerable suffering.

When I identify with the story of my relationship with my father, poignant memories of our shared adventures arise. I feel sweet sorrow. I wish I had appreciated him more. I feel disappointed. I can meander along in reverie about my father. But when I step back, I see that particular thoughts create particular moods.

This is the direction of investigation: to watch closely the network of connections and to see which of them lead to contentment and which do not. In this way, taking a step back from content, mindfulness coupled with investigation begins to reveal to us how we have been creating trouble for ourselves unawares.

Redefining Investigation

I often went fishing with my father. It was there that I developed an appreciation for pausing, waiting, patience. Fishing requires settling back and giving up control. The line is in the water. Maybe something comes to visit, maybe not. However, there is keen attention to the slightest movement at the end of the fishing pole. How it moves and the pattern of that movement matter. If it's an eel, there is one strong, enduring drag on the line. A catfish or bass gives intermittent tugs. A pickerel gives a first pull; then the line goes soft for a bit. The fish is holding the bait lightly, taking it to a comfortable spot. You have to let the line run. Then the pickerel yanks. That's when *you* yank. If you pull the pole at the first tug, you lose the fish. It is critical to first step back and notice the context, not just react impulsively.

The Buddhist notion of investigation involves noticing the shifts in the field of experience, getting curious about the subtle pushes and pulls, noticing what feelings and thoughts come to visit and the effect they have on the breath and the body, the subtleties of cause and effect. When the body is tense, the mind does not easily relax. If I am cranky, the whole world seems irritating.

Some of what we see is predictable, and we are easily bored. Familiarity breeds habituation and even contempt at times. We stop seeing with fresh eyes. We want something more entertaining and fly away into fantasy. In fact, many of the Buddha's instructions were encouragements to look more deeply and consistently into the ordinary, to become more interested in the mundane. There are secrets here in the predictable, but we need to become curious before they will be revealed. Only then will we discover the self-created causes of suffering and the self-created causes of contentment.

In this type of investigation, attention is not primarily on content, on the particular fish swimming in the aquarium and what it reminds you of. Rather, it is on the changing patterns in the internal landscape and the interactive nature of experience. For example, when I was twelve, I played a game when I got into bed. After allowing my mind to drift for a while, I would pause and see if I could trace back the series of thoughts that led to the most recent thought. In effect, I was following the bread crumbs of cause-and-effect thoughts. I also noticed when emotions arose after particular thoughts. This is an example of the kind of investigation we are embarking on in meditation. It involves stepping back from content.

Shared Qualities of Experience

Buddhist meditators discovered that there are three characteristics that we all experience:

Dukkha: dissatisfaction, dis-ease: the axle on the cart not fitting snugly into the wheel well.

Anicca: impermanence on every level.

Anatta: lack of an enduring, unchanging, inherent self.

Insights into these characteristics are the gateway to greater ease and freedom, and such insights are said to naturally arise and deepen as mindfulness, coupled with engaged interest, develops. Traditionally *dukkha* is approached first. This is, after all, the heart of the matter in Buddhist psychology. The Buddha saw himself as a physician, intent on healing, supporting practitioners in investigating the causes of their suffering and discovering along the way the causes of happiness. In order to be free of dissatisfaction, we need to look more closely to see how we are cocreating it.

However, this is a particularly difficult investigation for Westerners. To be fair, it's challenging for all beings. We are not wired to move closer to what is uncomfortable. The idea of delayed gratification—that we must move closer to suffering in order to alleviate it—is just that, an idea. Our deep mind-set of survival of the fittest begs to differ.

This is the great challenge of psychotherapy. Clients come to get rid of discomfort, not get closer to it. Who am I to say you should get closer to your pain that you have been avoiding your whole life? Granted, your avoidance hasn't worked, or you wouldn't be in my office. But maybe I know a more effective way to help you bypass this difficulty. My job is to create a holding environment of sufficient safety and trust, because only in that context might you feel encouraged to explore the darker side of the moon.

The Buddha understood that in order to gain relief from

suffering, we have to first become more familiar with it, see it in operation up close and personal. In the old days, it was more difficult to avoid the existential realities—sickness, old age, and death. Maybe in the Buddha's day it was customary to look directly at dissatisfaction. Lifespan was half of what it is currently. Infant deaths were frequent and even commonplace. Monks were encouraged to meditate in cemeteries, where corpses could be seen in various stages of decay. We, however, have become skillful at keeping suffering out of sight. And when it comes to meditation practice, we prefer not to look too closely at dis-ease.

Because of our strong aversion to working with mental suffering, we will first examine impermanence. All things pass. The concept of impermanence, though challenging in its own right, is a concept that is familiar to us. We were all children once, but no longer. And who among us has not experienced loss? We will start here, slowly, with the unstable, changing nature of experience and our uneasy relationship to it.

QUESTIONS FOR CONSIDERATION

I get confused about this new way of investigating. Does thinking stop completely when investigation is happening?

Only the far-flung and analytical thinking diminishes as one begins to notice more closely what is going on in the moment and observe connections between this moment and the previous or next experience. For example, in the treatment of anxiety, we know that anxious thoughts and feelings cannot coexist with relaxed, diaphragmatic breathing. This in itself can be a useful mindful investigation. Come and see this for yourself (*ehipassiko*). When you are restless or agitated, check to see how the breath is. Spoiler alert: it is probably not relaxed. Tense, shallow breath and irritable thoughts and feelings arise together and co-condition one another. This is investigation in the mindful sense.

You are noticing cause-and-effect links, in this case between the body and the mind. And it works both ways. Tense breath tends to invite tense thoughts and feelings, but irritable thoughts will constrict the breath. You can also diffuse this unwholesome dynamic in either direction. You can intentionally invite again the holding environment by either shifting to more pleasant thoughts or images, or by intentionally softening the breath. Simply being mindful of the tension in both the mind and the breath, however, without this kind of investigation and intentional reset, is likely to be tiresome and frustrating. This is why mindfulness without investigation will not necessarily reduce suffering.

I always thought mindfulness was just being present to one thing after another, with acceptance if possible. It seems like investigation is adding another more active element here. Do I have that right?

Yes. Now that we have learned to settle down, calm down, and get engaged in our internal landscape, the next step is to see how things are interconnected in there and, in particular, what contributes to mental distress and what leads toward contentment. The direction of these practices has always been toward reducing self-created mental distress, and this is a proactive process. We have to look closely at how this is happening so that we can develop new and helpful ways of holding, shaping, and responding to our experience. That is why calming down or being generally mindful, while necessary and important in their own right, will not help us understand the causes of suffering and the causes of abiding contentment. Investigation is not emphasized in many mindfulness instructions because it is assumed that this will arise on its own. But it doesn't for many of us, though it is critical for the deepening of insight.

15

RISING AND
FALLING GAMES

So you should view this fleeting world as a star at dawn, a
bubble in a stream, a flash of lightning in a summer cloud, a
flickering lamp, a phantom and a dream.

—Gautama Buddha

No man ever steps in the same river twice, for it's not the
same river and he's not the same man.

—Heraclitus

AT FIRST BLUSH, IT MIGHT SEEM THAT BOTH the Buddha and
Heracleitus had an incredible grasp of the obvious. We all know
that things change. It's common knowledge. People die. Yet seeing
deeply into impermanence is considered a pivotal insight in mindfulness practice. At times, the Buddha got pretty emphatic in his
emphasis on this. He once suggested that it was more transformative to have one moment of penetrating insight into impermanence
than one hundred years of noble conduct. Why is insight into impermanence so pivotal here?

Although we have a general understanding of the changing
nature of experience, we *behave* as if things are relatively stable.
The world is spinning on its axis, but do we notice? Our eyes are

in constant motion, yet the landscape before us appears in steady focus. Our neurological wiring has developed to support this relative view of stability in our perception and a sense of continuity over time through memory. These developments allow us to communicate and negotiate the world we live in. They represent incredible developmental achievements.

So what's the problem with a perception of stability? Why would I want to tamper with a pinnacle of human development? The American poet Muriel Rukeyser writes, "The universe is made of stories, not of atoms."[1] This is a large part of how we make meaning in our relationships and in our world. The problem lies in the fact that we forget that our meaning making, our stories, are constructed by our minds moment to moment.

As we reflect on our perceptions more deeply, we can see that nothing in our experience lasts for more than a fleeting moment. We need look no further than each exhale of our breath for evidence of this truth: once it's finished, that same exhale can never be retrieved or experienced again. It is the mind that rapidly organizes and synthesizes our ongoing fire hose of experience, much of which takes place under the radar of our awareness.

Because we are not in touch with the fundamental underpinnings of impermanence, we become strongly attached to our lovely but fleeting constructions. This attachment to a sense of permanence creates mental suffering (*dukkha*) when we face the reality of change.

With mindfulness practice, we become increasingly aware of the moment-to-moment constructing process. This goes against the grain of our neurological wiring, our cultural conditioning, and our personal attachments. We are swimming upstream here.

That is precisely why the willingness to look steadily at impermanence, our closer investigation into this disarming truth, rests on the foundation of practices that are both calming and stabilizing. These prerequisite steps, the establishing of tranquility and the holding environment, are included in the first meditation below.

GUIDED MEDITATION: IMPERMANENCE

1. As always, as if for the first time, take a few moments to settle the body and soften the breath.

2. Establish the holding environment, arousing qualities of delight, gratitude, warmth, and wonder.

3. With each exhalation, imagine the energy moving down, releasing with gravity. Maintain relaxation of the breath, but with no particular object of focus.

4. Begin to notice some of the minute sensations of breath at the tip of the nose, in the downward flow of the exhalation, as if that flow were actually comprised of a few smaller wavelets and particles of sensation.

5. Now, with each exhalation, notice a few sensations as the breath passes the nostrils. What before was a flow of breath is now seen as many smaller sensations.

6. Imagine that these sensations are soothing.

7. Keeping the breath soft, begin to notice sounds on the inhalation.

8. Emphasize brief, precise noticings. If you stay with one sound, notice that it is comprised of many smaller, fluctuating nuances of sound.

9. Imagine that the sounds are compelling, sweet.

10. Begin to bring your attention to the impermanent nature of experience.

11. First, reflect on the fact that yesterday is no longer here. Whatever you did earlier today is gone. The memories that you have of those experiences are being known in the present moment.

12. Now observe that the previous breath is gone, completely gone, over the waterfall.

13. Zoom in. On the out-breath, notice several precise sensations of breath. See that none of them lasts for more than a split second. Look closely into this.

14. On the in-breath notice the rapidly shifting sensations of sound, none of them enduring.

15. At the end of each complete cycle of breath, notice that all of the sensations of breath and sound that you observed in that one breath are gone, completely gone, over the waterfall.

16. Check to see that you are settled and feeling calm, at about 4 energetically; continue to notice the impermanence of breath and sound from this receptive vantage point.

17. In the last few minutes of the meditation, let go of the precise noticing of impermanence, and relax into a general flow of soothing breath.

18. Take a few more sweet breaths before slowly opening your eyes.

The closer you look, the more fluid and changeable experience appears to be. At first, this is simply a curiosity, and when you stop meditating, the confidence in a relatively stable world naturally reasserts itself. With repetition, however, you gain clarity that this is not just a mental twist but reality, that experience is inherently in flux, changing second to second. Things are constantly arising and disappearing in rapid succession.

At a certain point of practice, this cognitive understanding becomes more deeply internalized. This is *really* the way it is. As that insight matures, it also becomes clear that you have organized your life without this awareness. You have been trying to replace impermanent bits of experience with other impermanent bits in an effort to be happy. This is indeed a poignant insight. With the deepening that comes with repetition, this insight is also freeing, as our tight and serious grip on experience begins to relax.

Good news alert: there is frequent misunderstanding about "letting go" or "detachment" in meditation, as if these practices could lead to a remote and disengaged relationship to life. For example: I won't be disappointed or hurt anymore because I will care less. Easy come, easy go. Why get attached when all things pass? This is not what unfolds. Rather there is a gradual adaptation to this new information about the pervasiveness of impermanence. As this happens there is a new adaptation, which takes the form of holding onto experience less tightly. This paradoxically creates space for more appreciation and gracious acceptance.

Next we need to look more closely into dissatisfaction (*dukkha*), caused by the axle not fitting snugly in the wheel.

QUESTIONS FOR CONSIDERATION

When I look closely at impermanence, I start to get anxious, which leads to restlessness and sometimes fear. How do I stop this roller coaster?

An insight that is obvious on one level but continues to deepen with practice is that all experience arises and passes away. Depending on how you are holding this insight up to the light, it can appear either frightening, poignant, or reassuring. The fact that things keep passing away in our experience, despite our efforts to hold on, can lead to feelings associated with loss of control, a sense that one is not in charge as much as one thought.

It can also enhance a sense of appreciation for all things lovely and fleeting. It can be reassuring in two respects: first, because even difficult mind states and challenging experiences pass, and second, as one experience weakens or dissolves, another arises.

As soon as mindfulness weakens, things seem to be permanent again, as if that were the default position of the mind. How can I stay more awake to the pervasiveness of impermanence?

Permanence *is* the default position of the mind. Our neurology is configured to create the sense of a solid self in a permanent world. This contributes to a sense of safety and security—to a point. However, because things are not permanent, a truth that rudely asserts itself repeatedly and unexpectedly in our lives, the mindfulness approach is oriented toward integrating the radical infrastructure of our experience. Why? So that we will not be so blindsided by its uprisings; so we can gradually establish a more harmonious and appreciative relationship with the fact that all things change and relax more in the midst of it.

I must admit I get a bit depressed when I even think about impermanence, much less when I meditate on it.

Sure, this is an acquired taste. It is important to honor our sweet wish for impermanence to not be so. It goes against the grain of our orientation to examine this closely. However, this *is* the way it is, and as we slowly move in this direction, it may become clear that some of our mental distress is associated with holding on in unrealistic ways and in making demands on life that are untenable. The difficult *and* the sublime moments in life all eventually end. And it is not just that things are dissolving; it can also be deeply reassuring to see that fresh experience keeps announcing itself, moment after moment, without cease.

16

"I CAN'T GET NO SATISFACTION" GAMES

THE OVERARCHING INTENTION of mindfulness training is to reduce mental distress. Most people have this in mind when they start practicing; they are looking for a quick fix, a way to feel better, often conceived as a respite from nonstop thinking and agitation. They have the sweet dream that meditation might transport them to a delightful space free from worry and concern. Perhaps mindfulness can be the means of excising unwanted thoughts and feelings from the psyche.

The dream is lovely and understandable, but it is one of the last holdouts of magical thinking. It can't possibly come true. We need to let go of this wish once and for all. We have learned in other arenas that the way to work something out involves first going into it more directly, not circumventing it. For better and for worse, the same principle applies in mindfulness training.

As such, we benefit from handholds and training wheels in preparation for the challenging work ahead. Approaching mental suffering gradually and with the support of the inner holding environment makes insight into self-created distress more accessible for practitioners. A common instruction in mindfulness is to simply "be with" mental suffering when it arises, which is much of the time, to notice it, label it, and not identify with or feed it. Most people, including myself, find this nearly impossible, especially early on in mindfulness training. We need a helping hand.

Obstacles in Meditation

Consider five classic hindrances that derail mindfulness practice. In my experience, the majority of meditators encounter every one of them.

Desire: The universal tendency to hold onto certain experiences tightly, wanting them to last. It implies strong attachment.

Aversion: Ill-will, anger, active avoidance, and a pushing away of experience are all part of this hindrance.

Sloth and torpor: Heavy, dull, sleepy, unmotivated, draggy, complacent, dreamy, drifty states of mind.

Restlessness or agitation: While self-explanatory, it can be shocking to discover how prevalent and pervasive and persistent agitation is and how difficult it is to settle down. Energetically everything over 6 on the 1-to-10 scale is in the restless zone. All that we identify as anxiety or stress falls in this category. This is pandemic in our manic culture.

Doubt: This includes uncertainty both about the usefulness and efficacy of mindfulness practice itself and about one's capacity to practice in a way that will bear fruit.

While it is important to label the various forms of mental suffering and learn new ways to manage, accept, or disengage from them, attempting to do this early in meditation is discouraging and overwhelming. Ironically, it often leads to *more* stress and dissatisfaction. That's why we first develop the holding environment as a prelude to looking at mental suffering. With that firmly established, now is the time to mindfully address and welcome unwanted and disowned thoughts and feelings.

A step-by-step approach is useful in most areas of new learning, and welcoming and mindfully negotiating difficult mind states is no exception. It's a matter of pacing for success. This may seem obvious, but it is not the common approach for working with difficult emotions. Suppose I begin meditating and am aware of agitation and restlessness. This would be quite common if I had not taken the time to first settle down and develop calm with the holding environment.

But let's say I just jumped into the meditation. I don't want agitation to be there. It doesn't feel good. So I give it partial, begrudging acknowledgment, hoping that will make it disappear. It doesn't. Now irritation shows up, followed by frustration. This becomes a self-perpetuating, vicious cycle.

How do we develop a more accepting relationship with the difficult thoughts and emotions we are inclined to avoid? We can learn to hold disturbing emotions in three steps. To understand this, imagine your consciousness is making contact with all your senses—seeing, hearing, feeling, smelling, and so on—in rapid succession. It is a nonstop flow of experience that is being monitored, filtered, and organized by consciousness. Sounds and sights and thoughts keep arising, tumbling over each other continuously. Yet even when we are settled, consciousness keeps doing its job. It never rests.

The ongoing stream of experience is continuous, and we are inextricably connected to it. None of what we experience lasts for more than a split second, but our neurological wiring tries its best to establish a sense of familiarity and continuity and solidity. Most of that occurs beneath our awareness. Mental suffering arises, however, when we intentionally try to hold on to some parts of experience and push away others, and get determined to take control and orchestrate our experience. This only leads to dissatisfaction.

While this may resonate conceptually, we are not inclined to look closely at dissatisfaction; we would rather look anywhere else. However for more than twenty-five hundred years, meditators have consistently reported the benefits of taking a direct look at the causes of mental suffering. So for the moment, try to suspend your skepticism in order to practice the guided meditation below. It can lead to a more direct investigation into the causes of self-created mental distress.

GUIDED MEDITATION: THE RIVER RUNS THROUGH US

1. Take a few minutes to settle down, quieting the body and breath, arriving more fully here in the present, glad to be here, wanting to be here.
2. Settle back in a receptive posture and notice that experience keeps arising all on its own. The heart keeps beating, the breath keeps moving in and out, and awareness of one thing after another keeps happening: now a sound, now a body sensation, now the breath, now a thought, now another thought.
3. Notice this directly. Stay with this until it becomes clear.
4. When an analytical thought arises, imagine that it is simply the next moment in the stream of experience and that it is not possible to step outside of that stream.
5. Now try to stop the flow of experience. Pay attention to what happens as you do this. Does the flow of experience stop?
6. Let go of that effort, settle back as much as possible, and relax in the ongoing flow of experience.
7. Take a few more easy breaths before slowly opening the eyes.

Inviting the Unwanted Guests

The next step of looking at mental distress goes against the grain. Now we consciously invite something difficult into our relatively pleasant inner holding environment. Who does that? That's the last thing I want to do. Now that I'm settled, why would I want to disturb the moment?

A technique in psychotherapy called *interoceptive exposure* can be highly effective in treating anxiety. In this approach, the client is encouraged to activate the physical symptoms of anxiety and use vivid imagination to arouse these intense feelings. In some cases the client may put himself in the actual situation that creates high anxiety. The goal is to eventually desensitize the person to the anxiety-provoking situation.

Obviously the client needs to have a very clear understanding of the rationale for this technique, and confidence in the therapist. With this approach, the client notices that if he or she can stay with the challenging evocative imagery, the anxiety, thoughts, and physical symptoms gradually lessen in intensity. The patient thus begins to gain confidence in his or her ability to lower an elevated level of anxiety and also discovers that with repetition, the mind begins to desensitize to the imagery that once caused great anxiety. Overall reactivity declines.

At one point, after helping a client get over a lifelong fear of elevators, I wondered why this approach was not taught as a meditation technique. Wouldn't it be equally effective in working with difficult emotions in meditation? And it is, I found. But like some individuals who suffer with anxiety, meditators are often not willing to take this initially uncomfortable approach. After all, it involves arousing the very thoughts and feelings they came to meditation to get rid of, once and for all.

For willing meditators, however, this exposure approach is especially effective if one has learned to cultivate a calm holding environment. The principle is the same as in working with anxiety. Usually, challenging mind states show up unbidden. They tend to hijack mindfulness and set in motion aversion, followed by strategies of avoidance, bargaining, partial toleration, and often discouragement. Instead, meditators can create a calm and spacious holding environment first and then invite an unwanted guest to the party, paying careful attention as they do so.

GUIDED MEDITATION: INVITING THE UNWANTED GUEST

1. Take a few minutes to settle the body and soften the breath.
2. Aim to bring your overall energy/anxiety to 4.
3. Bring to mind a situation, from the past or more recently, that elicits a moderate degree of agitation or anxiety.
4. Make the image as vivid as possible, bringing to the fore any uncomfortable physical sensations associated with it.
5. Stay as mindful as possible of the unpleasant thoughts, feelings, and sensations. Aim to bring the level of anxiety to 7.
6. Now let go of the imagery, and reestablish the calming holding environment. Bring the energy level back to 4.
7. Repeat this cycle three or four times. Carefully take note of any changes as you move through these repetitions.
8. In the last few minutes of each repetition, reestablish and rest in the inner holding environment.

The following exercise takes this work a step further. Rather than releasing the imagery in order to reestablish the holding environment, you try to elicit the calm state while staying with the unpleasant imagery.

GUIDED MEDITATION: TRANSFORMING THE UNWANTED GUEST

1. Repeat steps 1 through 7 above.
2. The next time you bring the anxiety level to 7, begin to

soften the breath while staying focused on the aversive
imagery.

3. With each exhalation, allow the stress and aversion to flow
down and out of the body and mind.

4. Notice that the unpleasant thoughts and imagery are
still present, but the mind and body are becoming more
relaxed, less reactive.

5. Aim to bring the energy to 4, but without letting go of the
thoughts and images.

6. Pay close attention as you engage this process.

7. In the last few minutes of the meditation, reestablish and
rest in the inner holding environment.

The first exercise develops the core skill of returning to a
comfortable home base in the face of adversity. When irritation
arises in the mind, have you noticed how it tends to proliferate?
Agitation tends to breed more agitation. One of the primary
sources of mental suffering stems from our inability to shift to a
more wholesome state when the internal landscape is stormy.

The second meditation develops the more advanced skill of establishing the holding environment in the presence of something
uncomfortable. We can't always shift to a greener pasture in the midst
of life's challenging moments. Learning how to reduce reactivity in
the midst of adversity is one of the high arts of mindfulness practice.
If you can have a terrible thought and not react to it by tensing or
averting, it loses much of its power to create suffering.

This final mental-distress game involves noticing what disturbs
or ruffles the calm internal holding environment once it has been
established.

GUIDED MEDITATION: TROUBLE IN PARADISE

1. Take a few minutes to settle down, quieting the body and breath.
2. Take your time in establishing the holding environment, inviting heart qualities of delight, gratitude, warmth, and wonder.
3. Deepen the quality of calm.
4. Settle back and begin to open to the flow of changing experience.
5. Carefully attend to what disrupts or ruffles the state of calm receptivity.
6. When some thought or feeling or physical sensation interrupts the calm flow of experience, stay with it or consciously return to it again and again, until you can maintain the state of calm even with the presence of the disturbance.
7. In the last few minutes, return to the simplicity of sitting and breathing easily.
8. Take a few more breaths before slowly opening the eyes.

Having now explored dissatisfaction and impermanence, we will turn our attention to the nature of the elusive self (*anatta*). This final characteristic is the most counterintuitive of them all. Paradoxically, insight into its nature is deeply rewarding.

QUESTIONS FOR CONSIDERATION

My reactions of reaching for something I want or pushing away something negative seem to happen so quickly. You say that this is part of our wiring and that mental suffering is universal. Then how can I stop it?

It's true that mental suffering is part of our wiring, and that is a good thing. From an evolutionary perspective, early humans had to rapidly identify danger, especially predators. We are wired to move away from physical pain and gravitate toward safety and comfort.

We have learned over time to apply the same basic approach to our mental processes. We tend to relate to negative thoughts and feelings as if we were pulling our hand away from a hot stove. But trying to push away our alarm creates an agitated internal environment that generates more negative thoughts and feelings. Furthermore, there is nothing inherently "hot" in our mental experiences; thoughts and feelings are only made hot by our *aversion* to them. It is not our experiences but our responses to those experiences that shape our mental states. Over time the mind sees this connection more clearly, undeniably, and begins to adapt in a new manner that is less reactive and stressful.

My mind works so fast that I wonder if it is really possible to slow it down enough to see the disturbing thoughts soon enough to do something different.

You're right. The mind does work very fast. The emphasis in these guided imagery games is on *calming* the mind, not *slowing* it. From this perspective we can begin to see two components to every moment of experience: appraisal and response. Yes, most of the time these components blend together and happen automatically. The unconscious makes a rapid assessment of contact with every experience of seeing, hearing, touching, tasting, smelling, or thinking. It instantly assesses each experience to be pleasant, unpleasant, or neutral, and initiates the corresponding reaction of moving toward the pleasant, away from the unpleasant, or ignoring the neutral.

With mindfulness, we can learn to be less reactive to the assessment of the experience and to respond in a manner that minimizes distress. For example, I am meditating on the patio, and a neighbor starts a home improvement project with a chain saw. My immediate reaction is mild irritation. I could expand on that internally, right? Instead I close my eyes, draw a few slow breaths, and imagine that the sound is a lovely, calming sound vibration washing over me. I have created a different response that eliminates my distress and completely shifts my relationship to this initially irritating sound. Irritation is in the eye of the beholder, and this can be transformed, without trying to slow the mind.

I sometimes worry that I might get stuck in a negative state. Can this happen?

One of the liberating insights in this practice is the discovery that even difficult mind states are impermanent. It is also empowering to see that we can tolerate these states more than previously, that they are not overwhelming. We can also learn to create the conditions for these states to weaken and disperse, to not take hold or hijack us so dramatically. Moving gradually and delicately in this area is wise however: slowly, kindly, patiently.

I was taught to be mindful of discomfort or negativity when it arises; just label it, be with it, and try not to get hijacked. Your style seems to be more gradual. I'm concerned that I might be avoiding some things if I take this approach.

We are wired to avoid pain and move toward pleasure. If we try to attend to something unpleasant too soon in mindfulness practice, it will be coupled with a white-knuckled response or bargaining in some form (e.g., *I will be with this if it helps it to go away*). I am quite familiar with the no-holds-barred approach to working with difficult mind states that you describe. However, there is so much going on in these states, including aversion, self-recrimination, and restlessness, that trying not to get hijacked is like trying to manage a cascade of negativity. The capacity to hold what is happening is absent.

Working with these states is very important, but it is an advanced application of mindfulness. I encourage a gradual process of regulating exposure to difficult or negative emotions so as to not overwhelm the system. Rather than completely turning away from difficult states or diving into them in an unbalanced fashion, with this approach you will be on firmer ground to work with future challenging mental states that will arise.

17

THE
MALLEABLE SELF

NOTHING IN BUDDHIST PSYCHOLOGY IS MISUNDERSTOOD as frequently as *anatta,* the doctrine of no-self. It leads to mistaken notions that the self is an illusion or the belief that if I meditate really well, the sense of self will completely disappear—as if that would be a very good thing. Where would it go? What would replace it? We wouldn't think it desirable if sounds disappeared, or sights or taste, so why would it be liberating if the sense of self vanishes in meditation? If the self is not an illusion and it does not disappear with meditation practice, then what is meant by "no-self"?

With minimal meditation experience, one can get corroborating glimpses of the first two characteristics of existence: impermanence and mental suffering. The truth of impermanence (*anicca*) is obvious in everyday life, and meditation on it simply deepens insight into this ordinary truth. Similarly, one can easily grasp that clinging to the desirable and avoiding the difficult brings mental suffering. We have all had experiences of persistent clinging and its tormenting sequelae. The concept of *dukkha* simply invites a more subtle inquiry into this matter.

The notion of the separate self being insubstantial, however, is not obvious in any way. To say that it doesn't exist or that its existence is questionable flies in the face of common sense. The presence of a self that perceives the world and responds to it is clear and obvious. It is the most constant presence in our lives. For better and for worse, it is home base.

There are two issues to be explored here. The first is to clarify what is meant by "no-self." The second is to determine its usefulness or relevance in the matter of reducing mental suffering.

Redefining "No-Self"

Once again, translation issues come into play. The term "no-self" simply is not accurate. Even after a great deal of meditation practice, nothing about this terminology rings true. In fact, my own misconceptions of this have created much additional *dukkha*! For many years, I thought that if my intention was strong, my effort consistent, I would see that there is no self and that this would set "me" free. This did not happen, and for many years I attributed this to failure on my part.

More accurate and clear terminology is "shifting self," "non-enduring self," "noninherent self," "conditioned self." The implication is not that this self that we hold so dear doesn't exist, but that it is simply not as solid as we would like to believe, that it does not stand somehow outside of or above experience, that like everything else it is a product of causes and conditions. The self is not a solid thing located somewhere inside the body. It is the product of a series of interacting processes—a composite, an amalgam, a fusion. Like everything else in our experience, it is more wave than particle.

The self is a developmental achievement. It arises over time through interaction with the environment. It develops through a series of processes and is maintained by perception, comparing, orienting, thinking, memory, and so on. A whirring fan blade is a good analogy for our sense of self. At a certain speed, the blade appears to be nearly still and relatively stable. However, there are many things in rapid motion contributing to this perception of stillness. Similarly our neurological wiring is working nonstop behind the scenes to create the perception of a stable, coherent self.

Even if this makes sense in an abstract way, you may wonder why it is worth examining more closely. Why would I want to investigate the insubstantial nature of the self? Won't it just increase anxiety? Not when you discover that it isn't that the self vanishes or that we become disoriented. What changes is that our relationship to the self becomes lighter. We discover that the self is pliable, malleable. I find it helpful to think of *anatta* as "malleable self" rather than "no-self."

What a relief it was to discover this! Of course the self exists. It's just that it is a fluid process rather than a fixed "thing." It can shape-shift according to circumstance, respond differently depending upon the situation, consider from multiple angles, make choices.

This perspective makes sense, and I can directly experience the truth of it. I also can see the benefit in increasingly relating to the self as malleable. After all, the self also gets stuck and rigid and creates imprisoning thought and feeling worlds, creates suffering for itself. The understanding of self as *malleable* opens the possibility that self-defeating patterns are also just that—patterns, not immutable bedrock truths. If the self is inherently flexible and fluid, these patterns can be changed. Rigid boundaries can give way to a more permeable membrane. Angry thoughts may arise, for example, but this no longer implies that I am a "bad person." In fact harsh, self-critical beliefs can gradually be viewed in a more compassionate light. If the self is truly fluid, why would I want to keep hitting myself with a stick? My partner and I remind each other of this perspective regularly. When one of us loses or forgets something, or speaks in a less than exemplary manner, the other says, "You are still a good person." A careless moment need not define or even constrict us. Gratefully the self, like everything else, is a fluid, ongoing construction. It is more water than rock.

It is a great relief to begin to experience more spaciousness and lightness related to the self. It is not the self that is problematic. It is the *seriousness* with which we relate to it. Mindful investigation into the nature of the self, like changing the oil in your car, supports the self to operate in a less sticky, more smoothly functioning, more flexible manner: *malleable self.*

The guided meditation below places the thought of self as the central object of awareness.

GUIDED MEDITATION: OBSERVING THE MALLEABLE SELF

1. Take a few minutes to settle down, quieting the body and breath, arriving more fully here in the present, glad to be here, wanting to be here.

2. Invite the heart qualities of delight, gratitude, warmth, and wonder.

3. Settle back, and notice that experience keeps arising all on its own. The heart keeps beating, the breath keeps moving in and out, and awareness of one thing after another keeps happening: now a sound, now a body sensation, now the breath, now a thought, now another thought.

4. Notice how the thoughts of self—such as "I am sitting here" or "I am warm" or "My hips feel tight"—also arise on their own, frequently, bubbling up in the internal landscape.

5. Imagine that this thought of self—the idea that there is a self doing the meditation, thinking about what's going on, orchestrating what you are attending to—is just another experience that can be observed.

6. Now a sound, a body sensation, a thought of self, a sound, a thought of self: notice how all of these can be observed.

7. If the attention gets hijacked by analytical thought, settle back, take a few easy breaths, and once again open the field of awareness, first to sounds and body sensations, and then to notice again the arising of the thought of self.

8. In the last few minutes of the meditation, settle back into the holding environment, aware of a few easy breaths before slowly opening the eyes.

The next meditation game is an investigation into the location of the self. This is something we rarely consider. There is awareness of the self much of the time, but we don't think to identify its location. In Tibetan meditation, looking for the "home" of the self—and not finding it—is considered an important practice; it deepens the intuitive understanding of the composite, constructed, fluid nature of the self.

GUIDED MEDITATION: FIND THE SELF IN THIS PICTURE

1. Take your time and proceed through steps 1 through 4 in the previous meditation.
2. Now move the attention systematically through the body to see where the self might reside.
3. It may seem at first that the self is located in the head, somewhere behind the eyes. Keeping the breath relaxed, allow the attention to move into that area.
4. Carefully attend to your experience. Does the self appear to live there? Does anything seem to be stable and unchanging in this area?
5. Move your attention to the area of the heart. Does the sense of self reside here? What do you notice? What do you feel? Does the sense of self appear to be stable, or does it fluctuate like everything else?
6. Gently and slowly, move your attention through the body. Notice that the sense of self arises, but it does not appear to have a home base anywhere.

7. Maybe the self lives in the mind. Where is the mind exactly? See if you can find a home base for the mind.

8. Notice how thoughts come and go, sensations come and go, the thought of self comes and changes and disappears and reappears again.

9. Look into this carefully. What if this meditation is revealing the way things actually are?

10. Stay with this a bit longer. Is everything constantly shifting and changing, or not?

11. In the last few minutes of the meditation, settle back into the holding environment, aware of a few easy breaths before slowly opening the eyes.

The orientation in these exercises is to see that the sense of a separate self continues to arise, that it keeps coming, like the breath and the heartbeat. Thank goodness for this developmental miracle! Where was the self when you were three months old? It hadn't developed yet! The self keeps us oriented to time and place, and continues to spontaneously organize new input coming from the world out there and the internal environment. Another side of this also becomes apparent, however: the self is not a solid, enduring thing that resides somewhere. It is a constantly fluctuating series of interacting processes. Gradually we begin to acclimate to this malleable nature of the self, which is more wave than particle, more verb than noun.

QUESTIONS FOR CONSIDERATION

Whenever I try to meditate on self/no-self, I get caught up in thinking about it, which is often more compelling than the meditation itself. Suggestions?

This subject readily hijacks Western meditators, and that is why I have discussed it toward the end of the book. The attention needs to be pretty continuous and precise to see deeply into this matter. However, wanting to see deeply creates striving, which in turn invites tension, which agitates the holding environment and constricts clear seeing of what is going on. All mindful investigations rely on a foundation of a calm level of interest, with self-monitoring to notice when the holding environment is being ruffled. When such agitation is noted, it is most effective to reestablish the sense of ease before proceeding. It takes a while to trust that more insight will arise from this posture than from striving.

Noticing the different manifestations of the self—"I am here," "I remember this," "This reminds me of," "I think I'm getting the hang of this"—is like playing whack-a-mole. Is that the idea?

Developing a playful approach to meditation is definitely helpful. However, discernment is necessary to determine whether this style of play increases tension. I played a lot of pinball as a young man. The games certainly held my interest, but they were highly arousing. What we are going for in meditation games is *keen interest* without the hyperarousal and the restlessness associated with competition and a win/lose mentality.

Sometimes it seems like the self is not there at all; there is just pure awareness of a sound or sensations of breath. Does that mean I am making progress?

It sounds like there is progress in establishing the holding environment and concentration. These are important forerunners of investigation. In these moments, the sense of self is latent. However, the goal is not to keep the sense of self in hiding, but to understand its wavelike plasticity and mindfully support its smooth operation. That is why, after the mind is quite settled, the next step is to slowly open the field of awareness. Mindful investigation can then observe the shapeshifting movements of various phenomena, including the malleable sense of self.

What am I supposed to do once I see that the self is malleable? It all feels like a game, because as soon as I stop meditating, I'm totally caught up again in my everyday mind, filled with attachments and dislikes.

Meditation on the malleable self is a gradual path, and internalizing this understanding more deeply takes time. After all, we have been strongly identified with the self for a very long time. Each time we practice, a small hole is poked in the understanding of the self as something solid. At some point it starts to appear more porous, translucent, and spacious, and your everyday mind will become more malleable.

18

INTERPERSONAL GAMES

WE ARE COMPLEX CREATURES. Not only are we comfort-seeking and meaning-making beings, we are social beings. Mindfulness practice, in order to grow deeper roots in the West and in the lives of meditators in our culture, needs to address all three of these core aspects of our nature.

The comfort-seeking dimension has been addressed in the cultivation of the internal holding environment. By consciously creating a safe harbor in the midst of turbulent thoughts and feelings, the holding environment not only creates the foundation for deepening meditation practice, it addresses our need for ease, delight, warmth, and relaxation.

While comfort is necessary, it is not sufficient. The Buddha discovered this after exploring deep, blissful states of concentration. Indeed, he found these to be more satisfying than sensory pleasures. However, these states did not last and did not offer deeper insights into the nature of the mind and mental suffering. This discovery led him to the deeper search for meaning—hence, the subsequent practices of mindful investigation and inquiry.

The social dimension of practice is addressed in Buddhist teaching through the cultivation of nonharm to others and to oneself. The principle of radical interconnection is a foundational tenet in Buddhist psychology; practitioners are encouraged to be diligent regarding speech and action in the world. There is also an emphasis upon *sangha,* which refers to the likeminded practitioners who are walking this mindfulness path in community with one another.

This interpersonal aspect of mindfulness meditation is becoming increasingly important in the West. We want to know about its relevance outside of formal practice. Will mindfulness practice have an impact in our interactions and the world of relationships? Will we feel and act differently as we move through the day? We live in an outward-facing culture, and these questions matter to us. In the early years, meditation was misapprehended as a form of avoiding life's challenges—hence, the expression "gazing at one's navel." Long before that, even Freud saw meditation as regressive. It was considered by many to be selfish, disconnected from life, isolating. While early assessments of meditation failed to appreciate the many psychologically rich aspects of mindfulness, contemplative exercises that do not translate meaningfully into wholesome and constructive patterns of behavior will not gain traction in this culture. Bringing mindfulness alive interpersonally is a challenge we must collectively address.

I initially believed that relationship issues were not as important as individual mindfulness practice. I was convinced that unsatisfying interpersonal patterns and intimacy issues would be taken care of, put to rest, resolved by sincere meditation practice. This would happen naturally. I would be transformed inside and out by mindfulness.

This turned out to be yet another unrealistic expectation of meditation. Wouldn't it be lovely if one approach—a single technique (or belief or person)—could take care of everything? I recall an early, telling example of how my narrow approach to mindfulness did not improve my relationships. For several years I had learned the value of counting my breaths, from one to one hundred, more precisely when sitting in formal meditation and more generally when engaged in activities in the world. The practice was dry; there was no holding environment in it. Yet I was convinced that this was the only way to deepen practice and that eventually this would lead to the freedom I had read about. I had an unshakable confidence in this.

While my partner was also a meditator and appreciated my diligence, she reminded me from time to time that my approach was limited. One evening, when we were having dinner with another couple, I was silently and steadily counting my breaths. Later she told me I had been obviously disengaged during dinner, which she found to be disrespectful. Moreover, I was so convinced that counting my breaths was the most important thing I could be doing, more important than fully engaging with the people at my table, that I ignored her counsel. It took me a long while to see that I could be technically mindful yet inappropriate. And I certainly was not deepening my relationships!

It is not uncommon for practitioners to get stuck in a style of practice that minimizes the relational dimension of practice and that attempts to bypass anything interpersonally challenging: self-doubt, a sense of unworthiness or unlovability, social awkwardness. In my experience, interpersonal mindfulness will not arise automatically as an extension of formal mindfulness experience.

How shall we address the social dimension of mindfulness? First, by acknowledging we are social beings. One of our core needs is that of being seen and acknowledged. "I am in here! Can you see me?" is a core communication in the West. We want to be seen, heard, valued. Along the evolutionary ladder, we learned that "if I see you, you are more likely to see me." I see this as the obvious starting point for mindfulness in the world.

My coteacher, Susan, and I have designed several relational games. In this first one, the instruction is embedded in the title.

SOCIAL MINDFULNESS GAME 1:
I SEE YOU: TRANSFORM EVERY TRANSACTION
INTO CONNECTION

The underlying assumption of this game is that everyone wants to be seen, even if this need has not been explicitly identified, which is all too frequently the case. Wherever I go, whoever I run into, the intention is to convey to the other that I am. We try never to have an exchange with someone that is absent this intention.

The game involves a great deal of mindful discernment and creativity, which is what makes it interesting. It is a puzzle. Just as a sense of interest is an important factor in formal meditation practice, so it is in interpersonal practice. Each person is wired differently. How can he or she be approached? Is more than brief eye contact perceived as intrusive? Is too much friendliness off-putting? What is the best way to say hello to this one? And that one? Appropriate use of humor? Discussion of the weather? People are often busy, preoccupied; how can I finesse a meaningful moment of connection in the midst of that busyness?

Sometimes it takes a few attempts. Consider a waitperson in a restaurant, for instance. There may be a professional, practiced kind of welcoming that is part of most service industries, but often this is superficial and somewhat harried. How might that person be seen and appreciated more fully, in a few brief moments? A playful, offbeat antic will often lighten the atmosphere and initiate a more relaxed flow of interaction.

This exercise is not simply altruistic. It capitalizes on a simple principle: just as the other wants to be seen, so do I. When a waitress feels seen, she sees me seeing her. I am the one who is proactively initiating a process whereby all of us may, even in a brief exchange, address this core need. It gets us out of our heads, changes our mood, and seems like a lovely practice to take up in this world-on-fire.

In the Tibetan Buddhist tradition, meditators are encouraged to imagine that everyone you encounter has been your mother in a previous lifetime. This can seem a bit of a stretch for Westerners. Whether one happens to believe in reincarnation or not, however, the purpose of this reflection is to increase a sense of affinity with our species as one moves through the world.

The following exercise is oriented toward breaking down the sense of guardedness and disconnection that often populates our interpersonal lives.

SOCIAL MINDFULNESS GAME 2: THERE BUT FOR THE GRACE OF CONDITIONS

1. As you move through your day, first notice someone who appears to be upbeat, smiling.
2. Imagine that the person has experienced something positive that accounts for this delight, has felt seen, admired, has known success.
3. Next notice someone who appears distracted, lost in thought, hurried.
4. Consider that this person may feel pressured, stressed, burdened by circumstance, unable presently to relax or access lightness.
5. Next notice someone who seems depressed.
6. This person may have experienced loss or deprivation, perhaps is isolated, filled with self-doubt, unable to access joy.
7. Notice someone who appears to be impatient, angry.
8. Reflect that this person may have known rejection, disappointment, unrequited love, and is unable to access ease and friendliness.
9. Perhaps we are all subject to causes and conditions that shape our disposition and outlook. At times you, too, have appeared to be upbeat, distracted, depressed, or irritable.
10. Notice someone else now. Imagine that you can see this person's life unfold in time-lapse photography, viewing

significant moments in his or her early upbringing, moving forward to moments of joy, moments of sorrow and loss, and then to what happened earlier today.

11. Whatever emotional state this person appears to be manifesting, does it make more sense now? Does it change the sense of connection with this person? Does it elicit a sense of compassion?

I also find it useful to bring relational mindfulness into retreats, workshops, and work with couples. The following dyadic exercise brings into focus a more subtle appreciation of seeing and being seen.

SOCIAL MINDFULNESS GAME 3: SWIMMING IN THE SAME AQUARIUM

1. Sit facing another person. Before you both close your eyes, decide which of you will ring the bell and open their eyes first. Both of you close your eyes. Take a few moments to settle in, soften the breath.

2. In a moment, one of you will open your eyes, ring the bell, and gaze upon the person before you. The other will keep eyes closed with the awareness that he or she is being seen by the partner.

3. Both of you can notice what happens in your experience as you prepare to do this exercise. Does the breath change? What thoughts arise? Are you aware of discomfort or anxiety?

4. Now, one of you open your eyes, ring the bell, and look at your partner. For two or three minutes, both of you mindfully check in on your experience. What is it like to gaze upon another human being whose eyes are closed? What is it like to be gazed upon? Can you open to this?

5. Consider the following: Just like you, this person before you was once young, a child, exploring the world, has known both joy and sorrow, has had challenges, has known success and disappointment. Just like you, she has had dreams; some have come true, some not. Just like you, she has known love and loss, the exuberance of victory and the pain of defeat. And just like you, she too wants to love and be loved.

6. The person with eyes open now rings the bell; both of you close your eyes and take two or three minutes to be with your experience. Prepare to switch positions.

7. The other person now opens her eyes and rings the bell. Gazing at her partner, the observer reflects: Before you is a fellow human being, sharing this precious and challenging life. Just like you, he has endured much to arrive at this point in life, has known joy and sorrow, acceptance and rejection, sickness as well as health. He is growing old just like you, wants to be more comfortable in his skin and in the world, wants to find a deeper sense of purpose, grow in wisdom and compassion, just like you.

8. The person gazing rings the bell. Both of you close your eyes and open to your felt experience.

9. After three minutes, open your eyes and share your experience with each other.

The qualities of the holding environment are important both on the cushion and off. The more we develop these qualities in formal practice, the more they begin to show up in our day-to-day lives. Letting go of detailed mindfulness is necessary in interaction, however; holding onto this can itself create tension in daily life. A softer, more spacious approach is called for. Interacting with others, with eyes wide open, is complex and also calls for self-compassion. We are not simply watching people from a distance in these exercises. As participant-observers, we have our own triggers and vulnerabilities, our own interpersonal disappointments and needs to be seen. Being generous with ourselves and appreciating our intention is beneficial in any interaction.

These are a few suggestions for bringing your mindfulness practice from your meditation room into the relational domain. We are all in the same aquarium but often forget it. Mindfulness can remind us of our inherent connection with our fellow sentient beings. As always, I recommend that you be creative and find personally meaningful games in this area. They can brighten and enrich your daily interactions.

QUESTIONS FOR CONSIDERATION

What should I do when my buttons get pushed by someone who is self-centered, arrogant, or aggressive?

Like every other aspect of practice, we consider a graded hierarchy, moving from simpler to more challenging scenarios. There are situations and people more likely to trigger us, but we leave those for later. It's best to begin practicing in the shallow end of the pool. In this case we start with people who are either upbeat or neutral, those less likely to arouse negative feelings in us. So much of our experience falls in the casual or neutral category, and it is here that much of our formal meditation practice and mindful interaction with the world can be consciously brightened and enhanced. Gradually we can be less triggered even by those with challenging personality styles.

AFTERWORD:
KISS THE JOY AS IT FLIES

He who binds to himself a joy
Does the winged life destroy;
But he who kisses the joy as it flies
Lives in eternity's sunrise.

—Willam Blake

IN PSYCHOTHERAPY, a primary component and focus of the first session with a new client is to establish a welcoming, trustworthy environment, such that he or she will feel safe and sufficiently comfortable to return. As this trust in the holding environment deepens, the client becomes more willing to explore, reveal, and in time, open to ever-deepening reflection and revelation.

In similar fashion, Westerners need to feel this sense of comfort and safety early on in meditation. If this is not a priority, they are more likely to abandon the practice, and if they do continue, it may be an intermittent, frustrating, cognitive grind.

We need to take baby steps that make sense and feel good, steps that are appropriate to our cultural context. This is largely uncharted territory for us, and acknowledging that is an important first step—not an easy one in a cultural milieu that views "not knowing" as an admission of weakness.

The days of throwing a child into the water as a way of teaching him or her how to swim are over. Isn't it time we stop approaching meditation that way, too? Granted, the sticks in the meditation hall have been put away; this is no longer being seen as a useful motivational tool. But meditation is often still perceived as rather a dry and serious enterprise, good medicine at best.

Why aren't *you* meditating more regularly? Is it because you have not found it to be refreshing? Or perhaps because you feel yourself to be a failure at it? Do you often feel you are barely managing restlessness and distraction until the bell rings?

Following the sensations of the breath is simply not terribly interesting. We need to find ways to infuse interest and creativity into what is essentially a repetitive, lifelong rhythm—not unlike the beating of our hearts.

But we are not generally encouraged to be creative in that way. We are not encouraged to actively soften and enliven the body and breath and heart. We are instructed to be with the breath as it is. If it is boring, then we should be with boredom. These instructions, by and large, are far too dry.

Interest is the mother of tranquil concentration, and tranquil concentration is the mother of insight. We must therefore create the conditions to foster and encourage interest right from the start. We must put our active minds to good use by cultivating calm, by engaging the heart, by discovering enriching, personally meaningful inroads in meditation. We can only do this if we find these "preliminary" practices to be useful in and of themselves. Only then can they lay the foundation for deeper exploration, insight, and a sense of true inner peace and well-being.

So much is written about happiness these days. We all want contentment but often look for it in the wrong places. Even if we understand that happiness is not to be found in a bigger house or faster car, we still overschedule, overconnect, overeat, underexercise, and have few abiding, available inner resources for managing stress.

Mindfulness, practiced in the right way, directly contributes to this core need for well-being. It suggests that with appropriate, engaging attention we can learn how to cultivate beneficial states of mind and heart. We can learn to be less driven by desires and urges that we often intuitively know detract from our integrity and wholeness. As we come to understand these patterns that inhibit—and even *prohibit*—our growth and potential happiness, we can begin to unravel the "ties that bind us" and relax into a more spacious inner landscape and a far more comfortable existence in the world we share. From my retreat journal:

> Mindfulness takes practice in the way that love
> takes practice,
> in the way that enjoying a sunset takes practice,
> or empathizing with a dear friend,
> or listening, with a sense of wonder,
> to the sound of the ocean in a conch shell.

There is a wonderful encapsulated expression of happiness in Japanese Morita therapy. *Aru ga mama* means "that state where the mind is not unduly disturbed by anything and runs smoothly." I find this to be deceptively simple and elegant. "Not unduly disturbed by anything" implies an extremely welcoming posture of mind. This isn't the same as "previously challenging things no longer come to visit." It suggests that the mind is at home with whatever arises.

I once studied with a venerable Burmese monk who graciously offered the following instruction to me. I am forever indebted to him and will remember his words always:

> Your practice is becoming fluid, but there are a few spots which are rough. As monks we only have our robes, and we learn to stitch them when they tear. When you use a rusty needle, the needle catches on the cloth when it passes through the material. But when you use a clean needle, it does not catch on the cloth. Focus on where the needle is

catching on the cloth and what you can do to clean it. The less the needle of mindfulness catches on the cloth of experience, the more you will experience happiness and freedom.

In closing, these are my words, my hope, for you—which is to say, for us all:

> May you create delight in your meditation.
> May your mind not be unduly ruffled by anything;
> may it not catch on the cloth of your experience.
> May the mind, having struggled for so long trying
>   to make things other than what they are,
> rest lightly in the trustworthy stream of experience.

NOTES

Chapter 2. Different Strokes

1. "The Quotations Page: Quote from Mahatma Gandhi." *The Quotations Page,* www.quotationspage.com/quote/4013.html (accessed August 31, 2015).
2. Jon Kabat-Zinn, *Wherever You Go There You Are: Mindfulness Meditation in Everyday Life* (New York: Hyperion, 1994), 4.
3. Dilgo Khyentse Rinpoche, *Zurchungpa's Testament: A Commentary on Zurchung Sherab Trakpa's Eighty Chapters of Personal Advice* (Ithaca, NY: Snow Lion, 2006), 204.
4. Tara Brach, *Radical Acceptance: Embracing Your Life with the Heart of a Buddha* (New York: Bantam Dell, 2003), 3.

Chapter 3. The Inner Holding Environment

1. Bruce E. Wampold, *The Great Psychotherapy Debate: Models, Methods, and Findings* (Mahwah, NJ: L. Erlbaum Associates, 2004).
2. David Schneider, *Crowded by Beauty: The Life and Zen of Poet Philip Whalen* (Oakland, CA: University of California Press, 2015).

Chapter 5. Relaxation

1. "Maha-Saccaka Sutta: The Longer Discourse to Saccaka" (MN 36), translated from the Pali by Thanissaro Bhikkhu, from *Access to Insight,* www.accesstoinsight.org (accessed August 31, 2015).

Chapter 6. Playfulness and Delight

1. D. W. Winnicott, *Playing and Reality* (New York: Basic Books, 1971), 38.

Chapter 7. Gratitude and Wonder

1. Dhammapada 2, from Thanissaro Bhikkhu, trans., *Dhammapada: A Translation* (Barre, MA: Dhamma Dana Publications, Barre Center for Buddhist Studies, 1998). I have changed the word *heart* in his translation to *mind.*

Chapter 10. Tranquility Games

1. *Oxford Dictionary of English, 3rd ed.* (Oxford, UK: Oxford University Press, 2010).
2. Mary Oliver, "When Death Comes," *New and Selected Poems* (Boston: Beacon Press, 1992), 8.

Chapter 15. Rising and Falling Games

1. Muriel Rukeyser, "The Speed of Darkness," *The Collected Poems of Muriel Rukeyser* (Pittsburgh, PA: University of Pittsburgh Press, 2005), 467.

BIBLIOGRAPHY

Aronson, Harvey. *Buddhist Practice on Western Ground: Reconciling Eastern Ideals and Western Psychology*. Boston: Shambhala Publications, 2004.

Batchelor, Stephen. *Buddhism without Beliefs*. New York: Riverhead Books, 1997.

Bays, Jan Chozen. *How to Train a Wild Elephant and Other Adventures in Mindfulness*. Boston: Shambhala Publications, 2011.

Beck, Charlotte Joko. *Everyday Zen: Love and Work*. San Francisco: HarperSanFrancisco, 1989.

Bhikkhu Ñāṇamoli and Bhikkhu Bodhi. 2009. *The Middle Length Discourses of the Buddha: A Translation of the Majjhima Nikaya*. Somerville, MA: Wisdom Publications.

Brach, Tara. *Radical Acceptance: Embracing Your Life with the Heart of a Buddha*. New York: Bantam Dell, 2003.

———. *True Refuge: Finding Peace and Freedom in Our Own Awakened Heart*. New York: Bantam Books, 2012.

Chödrön, Pema. *The Wisdom of No Escape and the Path of Loving-Kindness*. Boston: Shambhala Publications, 2001.

———. *Taking the Leap: Freeing Ourselves from Old Habits and Fears*. Boston: Shambhala Publications, 2009.

The Dalai Lama and Howard Cutler. *The Art of Happiness: A Handbook for Living*. New York: Riverhead Books, 1998.

Epstein, Mark. *Thoughts without a Thinker: Psychotherapy from a Buddhist Perspective.* New York: Basic Books, 1995.

———. *Going to Pieces without Falling Apart: A Buddhist Perspective on Wholeness.* New York: Broadway Books, 1998.

———. *Psychotherapy without the Self: A Buddhist Perspective.* New Haven, CT: Yale University Press, 2007.

———. *The Trauma of Everyday Life.* London: Penguin Random House, 2013.

Fronsdal, Gil. *The Dhammapada: Teachings of the Buddha.* Boston: Shambhala Publications, 2008.

Germer, Christopher. *The Mindful Path to Self-Compassion: Freeing Yourself from Destructive Thoughts and Emotions.* New York: Guilford, 2009.

Germer, Christopher, and Ronald Siegel, eds. *Wisdom and Compassion in Psychotherapy: Deepening Mindfulness in Clinical Practice.* New York: Guilford, 2012.

Germer, Christopher, Ronald Siegel, and Paul Fulton, eds. *Mindfulness and Psychotherapy,* second edition. New York: Guilford, 2013.

Gilbert, Jack. *Refusing Heaven: Poems.* New York: Knopf, 2005.

Gilbert, Paul. *Compassion: Conceptualisations, Research and Use in Psychotherapy.* London: Routledge, 2005.

———. *The Compassionate Mind: A New Approach to Life's Challenges.* Oakland, CA: New Harbinger Press, 2009.

Goldstein, Joseph. *Insight Meditation: The Practice of Freedom.* Boston: Shambhala Publications, 1993.

———. *One Dharma: The Emerging Western Buddhism.* San Francisco: HarperSanFrancisco, 2002.

———. *Mindfulness: A Practical Guide to Awakening.* Boulder, CO: Sounds True, 2013.

Goldstein, Joseph, and Jack Kornfield. *Seeking the Heart of Wisdom.* Boston: Shambhala Publications, 1987.

Goleman, Daniel, and the Dalai Lama. *Destructive Emotions: How Can We Overcome Them?* New York: Bantam Dell, 2003.

Gunaratana, Bhante Henepola. *Mindfulness in Plain English.* Somerville, MA: Wisdom Publications, 2002.

Hanh, Thich Nhat. *The Miracle of Mindfulness.* Boston: Beacon Press, 1975, 1987.

Kabat-Zinn, Jon. *Full Catastrophe Living.* New York: Delacorte Press, 1990.

———. *Wherever You Go There You Are: Mindfulness Meditation in Everyday Life.* New York: Hyperion, 1994.

———. *Coming to Our Senses: Healing Ourselves and the World through Mindfulness.* New York: Hyperion, 2005.

Kornfield, Jack. *A Path with Heart: A Guide through the Perils and Promises of Spiritual Life.* New York: Bantam Books, 1993.

———. *The Wise Heart: A Guide to the Universal Teachings of Buddhist Psychology.* New York: Bantam Books, 2008.

———. *Bringing Home the Dharma: Awakening Right Where You Are.* Boston: Shambhala Publications, 2011.

Kurtz, Ron. *Body-Centered Psychotherapy: The Hakomi Method.* Mendocino, CA: LifeRhythm, 1990.

Kwee, Maurits, Kenneth Gergen, and Fusako Koshikawa, eds. *Horizons in Buddhist Psychology.* Chagrin Falls, OH: Taos Institute Publications, 2007.

Langan, Robert. *Minding What Matters: Psychotherapy and the Buddha Within.* Somerville, MA: Wisdom Publications, 2006.

Magid, Barry. *Ordinary Mind: Exploring the Common Ground of Zen and Psychotherapy.* Somerville, MA: Wisdom Publications, 2002.

McDonald, Kathleen, and Robina Courtin. *How to Meditate: A Practical Guide.* Somerville, MA: Wisdom Publications, 1988.

Mingyur, Yongey, and Eric Swanson. *Joyful Wisdom: Embracing Change and Finding Freedom.* New York: Harmony Books, 2009.

Morgan, William. *Change in Meditation: A Phenomenological Study of Vipassana Meditators' Views of Progress.* Boston: Massachusetts School of Professional Psychology, 1990.

———. "Resistance in Meditation." *Insight Journal* (fall 2002): 29–33. https://www.bcbsdharma.org/article/resistance-in-meditation/.

Mruk, Christopher, and Joan Hartzell. *Zen and Psychotherapy: Integrating Traditional and Nontraditional Approaches.* New York: Springer Publishing, 2003.

Nyanaponika Thera. *The Heart of Buddhist Meditation.* Boston: Weiser Books, 1965, 1996.

Olendzki, Andrew. *Unlimiting Mind: The Radically Experiential Psychology of Buddhism.* Somerville, MA: Wisdom Publications, 2010.

Oliver, Mary. *Blue Pastures.* San Diego: Harcourt Brace, 1995.

Orsillo, Susan, and Lizabeth Roemer. *The Mindful Way through Anxiety.* New York: Guilford, 2011.

Pollak, Susan, Thomas Pedulla, and Ronald Siegel. *Sitting Together: Essential Skills for Mindfulness-Based Psychotherapy.* New York: Guilford, 2014.

Rahula, Walpola. *What the Buddha Taught.* New York: Grove Press, 1986.

Safran, Jeremy. *Psychoanalysis and Buddhism.* Somerville, MA: Wisdom Publications, 2003.

Salzberg, Sharon. *Lovingkindness: The Revolutionary Art of Happiness.* Boston: Shambhala Publications, 1995.

———. *Real Happiness: The Power of Meditation.* New York: Workman, 2011.

Schwartz, Jeffrey. *Brain Lock.* New York: Regan Books, 1996.

Sharples, Bob. *Meditation and Relaxation in Plain English.* Somerville, MA: Wisdom Publications, 2006.

Siegel, Daniel. *The Mindful Brain.* New York: W. W. Norton, 2007.

Siegel, Ronald. *The Mindfulness Solution: Everyday Practices for Everyday Problems.* New York: Guilford, 2010.

Smith, Jean, ed. *Breath Sweeps Mind: A First Guide to Meditation Practice.* New York: Riverhead Books, 1998.

Stern, Daniel. *The Present Moment in Psychotherapy and Everyday Life.* New York: W. W. Norton, 2004.

Stevenson, W. H., ed. *Blake, the Complete Poems.* London: Longman, 1989.

Trungpa, Chögyam. *Training the Mind and Cultivating Loving-Kindness.* Boston: Shambhala Publications, 2005.

Unno, Mark, ed. *Buddhism and Psychotherapy across Cultures.* Somerville, MA: Wisdom Publications, 2006.

Weiss, Andrew. *Beginning Mindfulness: Learning the Way of Awareness.* Novato, CA: New World Library, 2004.

Willock, Dee. *Falling into Easy: Help for Those Who Can't Meditate.* Washington, DC: O Books, 2012.